I0657578

SECRETS

Secrets

Copyright © 2018, Negative Capability Press
All rights revert to authors following publication.

Publisher and Founding Editor
Dr. Sue Brannan Walker

Assistant Editor
Jean Ahking

Layout and Cover Designer
Bailey Hammond Robertson

Cover Art
Jean Ahking

$21.95 (US)

13 digit ISBN: 978-0-942544-49-7
10 digit ISBN: 0942544498
Library of Congress Control Number: 2018952040

Negative Capability Press
62 Ridgelawn Drive East
Mobile, Alabama 36608
(251) 591- 2922

www.negativecapabilitypress.org
facebook.com/negativecapabilitypress

NEGATIVE CAPABILITY

At once it struck me what quality went to form a man of achievement, especially in literature, and which Shakespeare possessed so enormously—I mean **negative capability**, *that is when a man is capable of being in uncertainties, mysteries, doubts, without any irritable reaching after fact and reason.*

John Keats

CONTENTS

Letter to the Readers

Welcome to this volume of revealed secrets, dear reader.

Here, you will find a diversity: childhood secrets; family secrets—of mothers, daughters, and fathers; the shame as well as the desire of the body; secrets to living and to dying. Secrets are wisdom, joy. They can be an act, a theft, or a splaying wide open. Sometimes, secrets are subtle: the inner chanting of the mind. The secret is locked inside a room. And yet, they are opened in this volume, and tell of the ever-vulnerable life of the heart.

Once, they were tucked away, and had yielded a hidden, suggestive power, known or unknown by the owner. Yet, the act of making transforms them into the power of revealing and sharing, an intimacy between writer and reader. In these shared secrets, you will observe how they were realized in the act of writing.

But, there will be an intimacy within you as well. In the act of reading the secrets of others, your own, however dark or silly, will be suggested to you. Realize yours. May your secrets fester and simmer in ways that only you know. Then, share them. What's your secret?

I would like to thank Sue Walker, Editor-in-Chief of Negative Capability Press and Bailey Hammond Robertson, Book Designer and Typographer, for their hard work and dedication to this volume. I would also like to thank the contributors for sharing their deepest and darkest.

Reader, writer, tell all.

Sincerely,

Jean Ahking, Assistant Editor

GIANNA RUSSO

LAUNDRY

We watched all night but never found out who
was stealing Mom's underpants off the clothesline.

Before I could say what it was, I'd go in
the other bathroom and touch myself down there.

My best friend and I practiced kissing,
trading who was the man.

When Dad was out of town, Mom cooked us scrambled eggs
and hot dogs at 5 P.M., when she poured her first bourbon.

Burning trash, Dad caught the neighbor's punk trees on fire
and lied about it to the fireman.

We blindfolded the younger kid we hated
and made him walk through dog poop.

The boy across the street showed me his thing
and then we didn't talk to that family for years.

All of us had ringworm.

I got my first blood on a hurricane day,
at home, in baby doll pajamas.

ROBBI NESTER

SECRET

Remember the smooth plastic patch
between Barbie's legs?
I knew it wasn't really like that.
I'd seen my mother naked,
the barbed wire tangle of hair
that spoke of unmapped
territories I hadn't traveled to
just yet, places I didn't want to go.

I didn't have a Ken doll,
but I'd seen the zebras
at the zoo, black penises growing
and growing, like Pinocchio's nose.
And I'd seen my father too.
Every morning he'd take me
and my mother to the showers,
make us strip, and soap us up
under the spray, letting the hot water
wash us clean.

This went on until at eleven,
well-developed for my age,
I didn't look like Barbie anymore.
We were visiting the 64 World's Fair,
staying with a family friend
who stopped us in the hall
as we trooped, in towels, to the shower.

Her eyebrows rose and rose.
She grabbed me by the shoulders,
shoved me hard into the bathroom
by myself, and slammed the door.
I wondered what I'd done.
My face in the bathroom mirror

loomed, outsized and alien,
and I stood, suddenly awake,
a sleepwalker, about to take
a step across the sill. I saw
this body that was me,
wished it away, but it persisted.

From that time on, we never
saw that family friend again.
I showered alone, stuffed all
the keyholes with toilet paper,
ashamed of what I'd become.

ALICE FRIMAN

WHITE BLOOD

"Roses climb[ed] his life as if he were their trellis."

—William H. Gass

Of his diagnosis, Rilke writes only
of the cause: *the prick of a rose,*
recalling that cut on his left hand
while gathering roses for Nimet,
the Egyptian beauty. The initial
infection spreading from one arm
to the other. But who knows
how many years prior to that
stab and subsequent agony,
white cells began multiplying
in the corridors of his veins?

Imagine, Narcissus in spats
clutching the pain gnawing
under his waistcoat, running
a tongue over his mouth's
ulcerous sores. See how he
bends to the haze of his breath
lingering on the pool's mirror
as if like a rose or poem, breath too
demands to be committed to memory
before it lifts and melts away.

Roses in a silver bowl. Red rags
rioting the June fences, or upright
in a crystal vase. Roses delivered
in florist paper or stolen from
a neighbor's garden, but always

the glistening contradiction:
death alive in the bud, alive
in the terrible beauty
of the rose's bite. Could he
have come any closer to you, *Angel,*
than to this deepest self, pressed
in a book or left behind like a limp
reminder on a window sill?

When he said, *all soarings*
of my mind begin in my blood,
how could he not have known?
Twenty-five years before his death,
almost to the day, he paced the cliffs
at Duino—waves crashing the rocks,
bleeding out their white blood,
row after row pricked from within
by the white goad that rises in the body—
the thorn in the flesh wanting out.

Oh, what difference now.

To a dying poet, secrets matter little.
The high hour belongs to death:
the body's auger, the egg tooth
carried with us from the day we're born.
The white bit drilling its inexorable
way through the shell to the gift
we in our solitude always wanted to be:
the everlasting rose that mattered.

A LIGHTHOUSE LOOKED AT ME

We met at a friend's apartment in New York City the evening before my sister Ingri and I left for holidays in Spain. I received as a gift on that occasion from another friend a slim paperback edition of Ford Madox Ford's great novel, *The Good Soldier*, in which there is a sentence that captures the first time Kenneth and I looked at one another: "And it was a most remarkable, a most moving, glance, as if for a moment a lighthouse had looked at me." Although Kenneth was gentle, he blazed.

I was in Spain for Columbus Day and, returning to New York two weeks later, was engaged to Kenneth by Thanksgiving. I had been told that he lived in an ivory tower and ate Wonder Bread, but I found that the ivory tower was a boot camp for study, and the Wonder Bread (and Hostess Twinkies...) eventually became for me, as for Kenneth, manna in the desert.

The lighthouse continued to look at me and to enlarge and deepen the world.

WALKING ON AIR

Should I tell you
all things I understand
fill with the strange
information
of laughter,
that I am
happier
than I know?
I am sure I could
walk on air,
but my heart
is not trained
for that urgent
flight.
If life were all
stairs,
I'd have
no trouble
getting
around.

   I had always secretly known, but in time I discovered in words, that I was happier than I knew, at a depth that could not be tampered with. I remembered Martha Graham's certainty that with training, she could walk on air, and I thought about Saint Catherine of Siena's famous insight that Christ had made a stairway of his body for us to climb more easily to heaven. Many years later, meditating on happiness, I had the poem.

Snowshoes

We walked on
the Milky Way
that foamed
mirages—
pagodas
bristled
porcupines
swaying
silk on the high
seas
of elephants,
the snow a magnolia,
decked in its great
ivory lamps.

Powder snow foams underfoot and the Milky Way meanders across the sky. We're walking on stars, on the snow in the sky; the sky is under our snowshoes, and snow lies upon the earth. Shape-shifting shadows sheath and unsheath mirages. Every secret has been kept, every certainty is certainly something else, fabled and fabulous.

ALIAS STARDUST

As a player of games,
she knew how to be a toy
in an assumed body.
Sometimes she hid by being transparent
in several places at once;
sometimes she descended
through the brilliant
lights of the world,
stardust,
alias *stardust,*
a puppet
dressed as a girl,
beaten and
hanged in a chasm.

    Here she hid and assumed another body and became a toy. Her secret was that she was someone Other. Or she became transparent or a puppet who seemed to be a girl. She fell like stardust upon the world—she was a scapegoat. She was a star.

deKooning Grotesque

"Beauty becomes petulant to me," said de Kooning.
"I like the grotesque. It's more joyous..."

jackals cackling
haloes around their teeth,
forms somersaulting
inside zooscapes of rotten fruit
popping nooses
that I look through
like a lorgnette:

this pair of flying buttocks,
these brutal
burlesquing legs
under a venomous
swish of skirt,
this parasite and
zany of the stars,

ah, ah,
but to speak here of mother-love
is extravagant.

    de Kooning himself freely confided his secret in a marvelous precis—that beauty eventually became petulant to him, and he liked the grotesque because it was more joyous, more alive and energetic, more dynamic and gritty.
    Grotesquerie is a catapult into another dimension.

A DROP OF BLOOD

rises
out of the palm
of my hand
and sings falsetto into
my ear.

WALLY SWIST

A KIND OF THEFT

A dozen years ago I procured
        one of her two blue woolen hot pads
                as a keepsake for all the meals

I had prepared for her. Often, I had
        thought of giving the hot pad back
                to her during one of our meetings in

which she would display the light
        that she is able to emanate from
                her eyes and face. Over the years,

the blue woolen hot pad has lost its
        mystique, and has just become
                another *accoutrement* in the kitchen.

She being the one whose last words
        to me were, *I'll call you,* and who
                never has; although she dissembled

on one occasion, when
        she betrayed her usual facade by
                declaring, *we weren't supposed to be,*

not without an amount
        of impudence, whereupon a woman
                openly chafes against anything that

proves resistant in
        whatever context in relating to
                anything she considers as her freedom.

However, it was her blatant
    discounting of having
        a spiritual practice that proved to be

the most astonishing, as if she
    had abdicated the years of talking
        about her spiritual path, in her saying,

of course, I don't have
    a practice, so how would I know what
        enlightenment is, as if backing out of

having stood in that light
    whatsoever. Doing one thing
        and saying another may be indicative

of her high IQ, but it doesn't
    serve anyone, not even her,
        and even resembles a kind of theft—

giving one thing then taking
    it back, and then relinquishing
        the truth that she never gave at all.

Convenience in any
    relationship constitutes
        mendacity to the fabric of its very

nature. How I esteem
    the blue woolen hot pad now
        is by using it to take what is hot

out of the oven, and even
    though it was procured in theft,
        and from the ever so vertiginous

state of *amour,* never again may I need
    to suffer the lamentable experience
        of burning myself that way again.

RICHARD KOSTELANETZ

RELATIONSHIPS

Richard Kostelanetz: **RELATIONSHIPS**

I slept with EB because she proposed it; EB slept with me because she was curious about sex. I slept with BR because it seemed appropriate for a couple who had been seeing each other steadily for over a year; BR slept with me because she thought we would marry. I slept with ALT because she was the best-looking brilliant woman I had ever met; ALT slept with me because she felt in her synapses that I might be smarter than she was. I slept with CT because she was so blonde and WASPy; CT slept with me because her classmates taught her to desire something they called "experience." I slept with SB because she reminded me of Modigliani's women; SB slept with me because, as I remember it, no one else had made a pass at her in this new place. I slept with EAF because her size and energy made her so grandly seductive; EAF slept with me because, she said, my eyes enticed her. NW slept with me because she was collecting writers; I slept with NW as my marriage was breaking up. I slept with PW because she seemed so appreciative; PW slept with me because, as a publisher's new editorial assistant, she wanted to know writers better. I slept with JS because I had ogled her for years; JS slept with me because she had ogled me for just as many years. I slept with RJM because she was a published writer; RJM slept with me because I could, as a younger man, enhance her party image. I slept with BB because I found her charming; BB slept with me because she liked my company. I slept with LY because her rosy-cheeked complexion promised something I had been missing; LY slept with me because she felt lost in New York City. I slept with SO because I had been trying to do so for years; SO slept with me because she was no longer a virgin. I slept with AS initially because I thought her the most beautiful woman I had ever dated; AS slept with me because she loved me from the beginning. I slept with JU because she was "cute" and her eyes were imploring; JU slept with me as her one last fling before her impending marriage. I slept with KA because she was pretty in a conventional, "collegiate" way--very much like those girls who ignored me in high school; KA slept with me because she had already seen my name in print. I slept with RAR because she seemed such an adult child; RAR slept with me to impress her parents. I slept with MP because she had published me; MP slept with me likewise because she had published me. I slept with EL because I had been told she was good; EL slept with me because she had been told, by the same person who told me, that I too was good. I slept with LS because I remembered her as beautiful in her better days; LS slept with me because she remembered my liking her in her better days. I slept with BGS not just because she was incredibly skinny but because she also understood my art; BGS slept with me because she wanted to tell her mother back home she had settled down in America. I slept with JM because she lived nearby; JM slept with me for motives I'll never know. I slept with JS because I remembered her from high school; JS slept with me because she saw I was writing for the ~New York Times~. I slept with WJ because I was depressingly lonely; WJ slept with me because I seemed more stable than the other men she had been seeing. I slept with BS because she was a star; BS slept with me because, to my surprise, she thought me a star too. I slept with CI because she seemed the strongest, brightest college girl I had ever met--the superwoman of my undergraduate dreams; CI slept with me because she expected me to take her into the adult world. I slept with RNC because her capacity for understanding was so impressive; RNC slept with me initially because she sought a path out of her erroneous marriage. I slept with LV because someone so attractively slight could only be taken to bed; LV slept with me, I must admit, essentially because she was at the time promiscuous. I slept with JSM because no one else attractive at the beach resort was so visibly available; JSM slept with me because, dressed to be had, she wanted lots of sexual experience now that she was out on her own. I slept with SS because she was bright and well-kept; SS slept only with men she thought "classy." I slept with JC to see behind her perfect figure; JC slept with me because she liked, as he put it, "nonfreaky radicals." I slept with MO because she was so large and inviting; MO slept with me because I was over thirty. I slept with RC because she was so bright; RC slept with me because, she told me, "Knowing you, Richard, is an education." I slept with AT because she seemed so worldly; AT slept with me mostly because that evening she was drunk. I slept with FS because her art impressed me; FS slept with me because she was lonely and crazy. I slept with KM because she reminded me of a past love; KM slept with me out of profound discomfort with herself. I slept with AG because I had long known she was very, very intelligent; AG slept with me because I had just done something she hadn't--published a book. I slept with HK because I remembered her as the sexiest woman in high school; HK slept with me because now, unlike before, she was psychologically able to do so. I slept with DD because her body looked as though it would melt easily into mine; DD slept with me because her boss admired my activity. I slept with MW because she was so handsome; MW slept with me because she knew I thought her handsome. I slept with JAB because she was so picture-perfect beautiful; JAB slept with me because she was lonely, unhappy and insecure. I slept with NT because her perceptions were so strikingly acute; NT slept with me because I was the first man to invite her to bed in over a year. I slept with AD because I remembered her from elementary school; AD slept with me not just because she was recently divorced but also because she finally had herself fitted with an IUD. I slept with CF because I liked her artistic ambition; CF slept with me out respect for the seriousness of my professional purposes. I slept with MK because she made herself available to me; MK slept with me because she had purchased, though had not read, one of my books. I slept with JS because I coveted her diminutive body; JS slept with me because she could bury herself in my tummy. I slept with BK for reasons I cannot remember; BK slept with me for reasons I would rather not know. I slept with BBL because I had cultivated her when she was married; BBL slept with me because, now on her own, she was especially hungry for culture. I slept with HEB because I thought she looked both lovely and intelligent; HEB slept with me because she needed someone, anyone--even me--to carry her over her thirtieth birthday. I slept with AJM initially because she seemed so learned in areas I knew little about; AJM slept with me to hasten the end of her marriage. I slept with NK because I had fantasized about her for as long as I had known her; NK slept with me because her closest friends recommended me. I slept with HB because her face was so perfectly handsome; HB slept with me because she wanted an entree into the art world. I slept with MG because her athletic build and energy attracted me; MG slept with me because she had admired some criticism of mine. I slept with JW because she was wearing seductive clothing; JW wore seductive clothing because her employer published me. I slept with VA because she was a hometown girl in a foreign country; VA slept with me because here, unlike home, she preferred New Yorkers to the locals. I slept with CF because she seemed eager to learn about me; CF slept with me because she had thought me a famous writer. I slept with JF because I had long regarded her as attractive; JF slept with me because no one else was sleeping with her at the time. I slept with BC because I wondered if someone so sexy could really exhaust me; BC slept with me because she thought that she could push me around. DM slept with me because her husband had temporarily abandoned her; I slept with DM to assimilate her sophistication. I slept with SGW because she was so vivaciously flirtatious; SGW slept with me initially because I was fifteen years younger than her ex-husband. I slept with YL because she worked in commercial publishing; YL slept with me because she wanted to share my independence. I slept with SRH because she fulfilled an ideal that I later discovered was not at all for me; SRH slept with me because she loved me, I think. I slept with GM because I had previously seen her nude; GM slept with me because she was at the time collecting artists. I slept with WW because she was both voluptuous and bright; WW slept with me because, now out of college, she wanted to lose her virginity. I slept with RCR because her nipples were so protuberant; RCR slept with me because she wanted to meet my friends. I slept with EDM because she seemed so learned and smart; EDM slept with me because the lease on her apartment would soon expire. I slept with GF because she was so ingratiating, her imploring dark eyes bespeaking her sincere desire for me; GF slept with me because she found living in Staten Island so disagreeable. I slept with PG because she seemed so easily laid; PG slept with me because she was indeed an easy lay. I slept with SD because she was so fresh-faced pretty: SD slept with me because she was trying to put men, many men, between her ex-husband and the future. I slept with TT because she was the most elegant woman ever to accept a date with me; TT slept with me because she had heard long ago that I was an important something or other. I slept with FL because, once near the bedroom door, she fell so easily into my bed; FL slept with me because she wanted a place to stay in New York. I slept with RC because I had admired her writing; RC slept with me because no one else admired her writing so much. I slept with MHB because her movements were so spectacularly erotic; MHB slept with me because I was professionally productive. I slept with NM because I was trying to forget someone else; NM slept with me as someone to excavate her from her mother's house. I slept with FK because I found her so extravagantly comely and compelling; FK slept with me because she did not want to go home that night. I slept with GR initially because I thought her good-looking; GR slept with me to see if I would honor her highly particular sexual requests. I slept with DH because her light blonde hair turned me on; DH slept with me because her analyst advised her to do so. RAB slept with me because she had not been in love for years and desperately wanted to be turned on again; I slept with RAB initially because she earned twice as much money as I did. I slept with HG because she reminded me of fashion models; HG slept with me because someone sort of told her I was sort of famous. I slept with RFB because she did not protest; RFB slept with me because she felt that at this point in her life she needed practice. I slept with SB because she did not wear a bra; SB slept with me because she liked a certain essay I wrote. I slept with MA because she was so handsome; MA slept with me because, she told me much later, I was the first attractive man to try to seduce her in many years. I slept with RW because from first glance I liked her looks; RW slept with me because, after five years with someone else, she wanted to begin a new monogamous affair. I slept with JA because she seemed so smart about art; JA slept with me because, as she was always telling me, she thought me sweet. I slept with SOE initially because she had such a lovely presence; SOE slept with me because she wanted to discover if she and someone else, now me, could spend the night comfortably together at her new apartment. I slept with SM because she looked so smart; SM slept with me because she wanted to bust apart her second marriage. I slept with SC initially because she seemed both bright and sexy; SC slept with me because she found me affectionate. I slept with LM because no one else was flirting with me in a strange place; LM slept with me perhaps because, as she told me, she had remembered a poem of mine from her literature class, perhaps because of something else she was not telling me. I slept with ZK because of her exotic beauty; ZK slept with me because she was looking for a sugar daddy. SB slept with me because I was, amazingly, the first man to excite her since her marriage ended two years before; I slept with SB simply because she was so lovely. I slept with HD because she was a handsome Radcliffie; HD slept with me because her biggest enemy had already done so. I slept with MG because she was so hugely attractive; MG slept with me because she thought an affiliation with me would establish a base for her career in New York. I slept with TS because I had wanted to for years; TS slept with me because she had for all these years been unable to do so. I slept with BK because she seemed so curious about my work; BK slept with me because she wanted belated adult education. I slept with CV because her drawings were so sublime; CV slept with me out of the anxiety she might otherwise have regrets. I slept with KG because she initially seemed so beautiful; KG slept with me because she wasn't sleeping with anyone else, I guess. I slept with NK because I had, several years before, been moved by her presence; NK slept with me out of gratitude that her sexual attractiveness was not slipping. I slept with VR because she was so overwhelming; VR slept with me because she heard I was nice. I slept with MTD because she caught my eye at the fair; MTD slept with me because she wanted to add to her national chain a lover in New York. I slept with GS because she was the smartest woman there; GS slept with me because I was a member of the faculty. I slept with LD because she had the most extravagant breasts and lips I had ever seen; LD slept with me because she hoped I would be the man to change her life. I slept with PW because she propositioned me; PW propositioned me because she had no other place to spend the night. I slept with LG because she seemed so worldly; LG slept with me because she was trying to forget someone else. I slept with MW because she was bright and rich; MW slept with me because she liked my apartment. I slept with SG because she seemed much smarter than her friends; SG slept with me because I represented a world she wanted to know better. I slept with KW because she knew about art; KW slept with me because she wanted to revive her dormant artistic ambition. I slept with CB because she reminded me of JS: CB slept with me because she let her resistances lapse. I slept with CH because I had flirted with her several months before; CH slept with me because she had flirted with me several months before. I slept with PQ because a voice so enticing I wanted to hear as often as possible; PQ slept with me because, recently divorced, she was predisposed to sleep with almost anyone. I slept with MD initially because I admired the work she was doing; MD slept with me because she was curious about the man behind the by-line. I slept with CBS because she was so damned attractive; CBS slept with me because she liked men who made a concerted effort for her. I slept with MC as a precocious twenty-three year old; MC slept with me because she knew that I too was once a precocious twenty-three year old. I slept with TE because I had flirted with her 18 months before; TE slept with me because she thought me good-looking. I slept with CO because she seemed knowledgeable about sex--she was; CO slept with me because TE recommended it. I slept with FH because she was so pretty; FH slept with me because she wanted a substitute father for her sons. I slept with VP because I was to busy to do so several months before; VP slept with me because she wanted to, now as much as then. I slept with KF because she was so slight; KF slept with me because I reminded her of her father. I slept with RJ because for five whole years I had been dreaming about her; RJ slept with me because she wanted to marry, as her sister did, a native-born American. I slept with MB because she was so charming; MB slept with me because, now more than ever, she needed a man in her life. I slept with FS because I confused her with someone else; FS slept with me because she thought it would advance her career. I slept with GP because she had a superstar presence; GP slept with me because my self-confidence snowed her. I slept with WK because her voice was lovely and her conversation full of poetry; WK slept with me because she had checked me out in biographical reference books. I slept with JB because she had once refused me after she had teased me with an invitation to her house; JB slept with me because now she wanted to show up the men back home. I slept with RW because I imagined she'd be good in bed--she wasn't; RW slept with me because I lived in a loft. I slept with TV because she is taller than I am; TV slept with me because she wanted to see if I could succeed where others had failed--in curing her sexual neurasthenia. I slept with AG because I liked the image her art gave her; AG slept with me because she remembered a crush from high school. I slept with SN to solidify our professional relationship; SN slept with me for pretty much the same reason. I slept with BG because she was so petite; BG slept with me because I was twice her size. I slept with PI once because I wanted to see if her breasts were as good as they looked; PI slept with me only as long as she was high on cocaine. I slept with HA because she was so young; HA slept with me because I was so old. EM slept with me because I asked politely; I slept with EM because she had read all the best books. RR slept with me to assimilate mental muscles she wanted to develop in herself; I slept with RR to test her sincerety. I slept with DE to see if she was really as sexy as she portrayed herself; DE slept with me to generate experience she could use in her art. I slept with IS because she wanted me to do so; IS slept with me because she hoped through making love with me she could forget about living in the midwest. I slept with MJ because we couldn't fifteen years ago; MJ slept with me because we didn't fifteen years ago. I slept with LP because she moved her body toward me in a arc that caught my attention; LP slept with me to fulfill an ambition she made when we first met long ago. I slept with HB because she could smother me in her embrace; HB slept with me because my own hug was yet fiercer. I slept with MB because she was the most attractive woman among us; MB slept with me because, after her husband abandoned her, she needed to regain her heterosexual confidence. I slept with AS because she was so much older than I; AS slept with me because I was so young. I slept with AE because I loved her; AE slept with me because, she said, she loved me.

Philip C. Kolin

You Can Trust a River

You can trust a river
with your secrets.
A river speaks the language of silence
to protect voices even when
they are blindfolded.

Sinners have confessed deeply to a river—
betrayals and crimes
never to come to light in this world;
words from shriven mouths
stored in muddy vaults
and weed-anchored banks.

A river is also a coroner
stacking the secrets of rubbery bodies
on top of each other—
unweaned infants;
love-thwarted suicides;
black men lynched at sundown;
drowned fugitives; capsized sailors
with eyes gouged out
by garfish.

A river is the longest tear duct in America
filled with unshared sorrows
and lost dreams—pearls coated in silt.

A river never asks why.

A Short History of Secrets

Major diarists in the history of secrets,
they record mysterious messages in the sky
in fluttering, evaporating language.

War pigeons enlist in the espionage service
carrying battle plans and traitors' names
wound tightly around their feet

in crystal scarlet capsules
unraveled and decoded leagues away—
when words dare not travel by mouth.

A nightingale delivers hope about
an assignation to lovers barred
from seeing or writing each other

outdistancing parents
believing caging offspring
will thwart their escape.

Owls in wasted places
hearing unseen voices
impart knowledge

of the hooded future to seers
quilling predictions unfolding
continents and centuries away.

Divinations about empire
hide in the entrails of a hoopoe,
raven, or red-tailed hawk

until auguring priests
disembowel cuneiform fables
tangled inside.

God himself guards secrets
unless he glides into
the White Bird of Revelation

to announce the Parousia
to saints entombed in the catacombs
with flying birds painted on the walls.

Jennifer Lang

Seven Definitions of Secret [See-krit]

noun

1. *a mystery:* My monkey mind swings from branch to branch, alone, stranded in a primeval forest. My thoughts careen from one side of my brain to another, chafing my prefrontal cortex, guiding impulse control and judgement. My sporadic urge to bare my soul and tell all needs to be quelled. Who says some things are simply better left unsaid/unwritten anyhow?

adjective

2. *done, made or conducted without the knowledge of others:* Like a cartoon spy, I check over each shoulder to see if anyone is watching. Like a crook, I nab nuts—dark chocolate covered almonds, hazelnuts and cashews—and nibble. Like a discontented housewife, I circle the area several times to scan, snatch, munch and swallow. No resistance. No will power. No voice in my ear murmuring: stop. Only me pushing my cart, while bagging chopped walnuts, black sesame seeds and autumn-colored lentils in the bulk section of Eden Teva market, the closest thing in Israel I can find to my beloved Whole Foods in the San Francisco Bay Area. Only me succumbing to my id like a little girl who wasn't reprimanded enough to know better. Only me replaying my friend Alexis' words: "Sit on your hands if you can't control yourself with my cookies!" I rationalize that it's okay since everybody else tastes, too; since the store is so expensive; since I'm buying bread, fruit, vegetables, milk, alternative milk, eggs, pasta and smoked salmon. I wonder if this is considered petty theft or plain old theft; some deep-down, subconscious cry for attention, to test what might happen if I were caught or castigated; or, perhaps an attempt to jolt myself out of my midlife stupor.

3. *a. bearing the classification secret:* Some of the Israeli Defense Forces (IDF) top elite units: 8200, 504, 669 Search and Rescue, Aman, Meitar, Sayeret Matkal and many other names and numbers unfamiliar to me.

    b. limited to persons authorized to use information documents, etc., so classified: First my son enlisted in this select club after high school graduation in New York, and then my daughter was drafted after we moved to Israel. First my son donned a moss green, ground forces uniform and reported to an Intelligence unit, and now my daughter wears an Arabian sand-colored air force uniform and reports to the International Coordination unit. First my son shared little with us about his twelve hour days at an open base, and now my daughter measures her every word. First my son spoke in a hush-hush language full of codes and acronyms and expressions that I didn't understand, and now my daughter speaks half-English, half-army. My son, born in Israel on September 9, 1993, was four days old when Israeli former Prime Minister Yitzhak Rabin and PLO leader Yasser Arafat, alongside former President Bill Clinton, shook hands and signed The Oslo Accords on the White House lawn. My son (and any future children)—I had always dreamed—would never have to serve in the army. My son had other dreams. Sometimes I wonder what I could have done differently to make my dreams come true.

4. *kept from the knowledge of any but the initiated or privileged:* In fourth grade, I wrote a letter in my best cursive to my cherished childhood author, Beverly Cleary, telling her how much I admired Henry Huggins for having a paper route and related to Ramona Quimby for being called a pest. A few months later, Cleary wrote back, and I showed my teacher, then tucked the letter in my treasure box. In middle school, I obsessed over Judy Blume's young adult novels, reading one after the other: *Are You There God? It's Me, Margaret; Then Again, Maybe I Won't; It's Not the End of the World; Deenie; Blubber;* and *Starring Sally J. Freedman as Herself.* During my tween and teen years, I made weekly pilgrimages with my mother to the Oakland Public Library and opted for books like *Clan of the Cave Bear* or *The Color Purple* over titles like *Anna Karenina* or *Wuthering Heights.* In high school English class, I struggled to analyze deeper meanings and metaphors and loathed writing papers on *Lord of the Flies, Catcher in the Rye* and *The Stranger* so much that I often went to bed crying. During my college search, I chose a major in the school of Human Development and Social Policy at Northwestern University to avoid any English requirements. As an adult, I profess to be a writer but don't know the storyline of *Lolita, The Metamorphosis, Crime and Punishment, Moby Dick, Ulysses, The Iliad, The Odyssey* or other books that most regard as the classics. In my early fifties, I face a nagging question: am I a poorly-read writer—or worse—a poser, charlatan or sham?

5. *faithful or cautious in keeping confidential matters confidential; close-mouthed; reticent:* When my father phoned one Friday afternoon, his voice was matter-of-fact and muted. When he said, "There's something I need to tell you," I carried the phone upstairs to the master bath off my bedroom, the furthest place from my family, and locked the door. When he began babbling, "I've been wanting to come clean for a while…just figuring out when…but

then Mom and your brother found out so I had to tell you too," I clenched the receiver, awaiting the punchline: "I've been romantically involved with S. for twenty-five years." S., a high school drop-out, had worked as my father's secretary until he left law to work as a property manager and she followed. S., the primary breadwinner married to an unstable man who owned a gun, hunted and drank excessively. S., the mother of one son who committed suicide his freshman year of college. When I called my friend Alexis to sob, she said, "I'm so sorry," over and over to keep me on the other end of the receiver, to hear my breathing, to calm me. When I later collapsed into my husband's embrace, he made me laugh, saying, "You're so lucky. I've never had a secretary." When I phoned my big brother for support, he said, "This is their story, not yours. Don't make it about you." But, I wanted to say. But who was this man I used to call Dad? But what had made him take the less honorable path? When he was with us, was he thinking about her, or the other way around? Where did regret, remorse, repentance—feelings often born out of secrets—fit in, if at all? Why did he have to be so human, so flawed?

noun

6. *something that is or is kept secret, hidden, or concealed:* Goodie Two Shoes. Good Jewish Girl. Good Jewish Daughter. I never partied in the Oakland Hills, puked all over my bedroom, woke up with a hangover, snorted cocaine, broke curfew, snuck out of the house or was grounded. I never experimented with those vices because I had my own. I never succumbed to peer pressure because I surrendered to something else: under my hair, where no one could see, I dug my fingernails into my scalp, creating sores and scabs. After my mother confronted me, I denied it. After she dragged me to a dermatologist, who suggested Neutrogena's T Gel shampoo for dandruff and flakes, I used it. After the myriad pressures—good grades, college applications, job hunt, marriage—had passed, I stopped picking. After I recently detected one of my children constantly fiddling with hair, I resorted to my old ways, scratching at things that didn't itch, finding comfort in the motion, pondering the force of genetics, my failure to refrain, the gravity of secrets. Experts say: compulsive picking is a means of self-inflicted punishment or a method of deliberately causing the sensation of pain. Experts say: life has become so dull and uneventful that the pain is welcomed as a sign of actual engagement in the process of living. Experts say: the need to inflict pain is the distorted sense of relief that is realized when the pain (the picking) stops. Experts say: when this pain-inflicting behavior becomes a routine part of life, the relief from pain is felt only momentarily, at best. Does everyone harbor a private habit or surreptitious vice, and scalp scratching is mine? Do the brief pangs

of physical pain respond to or mollify my middle-aged restlessness? Do I feel fear of my father's past or just numb as I stare at my spouse of twenty-six years and our imminent empty nest and wonder what's next, not because I yearn for another man, but because I fantasize about another place, the golden city by the bay, home?

adjective

7. *beyond ordinary human understanding; esoteric:* Sometimes, after reaching orgasm, I sob, a deep, visceral, earthy sound that erupts from a mysterious well. Release. Relief. Repose.

WORSHIP

Even as a child
I always arrived
early to have an
aisle seat in the
pew by the 13th
Station where he hung life-sized, long and white, but for the blood
at his head, his right side where he was nailed to the wood. A blush
of lipstick that no nun could scrub away had seeped into the porous
plaster where women worshippers kissed his feet. Each time I put
my mouth above the spike to his cool hard foot, I thought of real
flesh and when the
others bowed their
heads, I followed
instead the arc of
his ribs, the line of
legs that even then,
O Lord, even then
I was lost, lost in
the beauty of men.

MARY S. PALMER

THE REVEREND REMINISCES

Two days before Christmas, following an altar girl with the cross held high, Reverend Timothy O'Malley walked down the center aisle of Saint Mary's Catholic Church. He moved slower than in the past. Knee surgery and his eighty-two years were telling on him.

Why am I still saying six AM Mass every morning? he mused. *I'm retired. I don't have to do this. Too many innovations nowadays. I never liked the idea of girls as altar servers but I have to tolerate them; I have to read some of the liturgy because it's been updated and my memorized version isn't in vogue. Hell, I can't even recite the Lord's Prayer anymore without stumbling on the words, embarrassing myself.*

Hell? I said hell on the steps to the sanctuary. God forgive me.

The deacon at his side held onto the priest's elbow as he walked up the steps and over to the lectern to face the parishioners. "In the name of the Father, the Son and the Holy Ghost—" The Mass had begun. As soon as Father O'Malley sat for the reading by the lecturer, his mind wandered again.

I guess it's the Irish in me; I always get sentimental at Christmas time and when a new year approaches. More so now that most of my family's gone and I never had a wife or a family of my own. I think about regrets. Over fifty years a priest. I've baptized many children, and their children. I've watched them grow up. Some turned out fine; others, not so good. I've buried many parishioners, too. And visited them in jail. Plus, listening to their woes and trying to advise and console them, promising them that God never forgets them. I've also reminded a few why they're on Earth— not to rack up millions but to serve God and reach Heaven.

He stared at the deacon who had begun reading the gospel but he wasn't listening to the words. He stroked the stubble on his chin. *I wonder what my life would have been like if I'd gone to medical school like I had planned? Maybe not much different. As an internist, I'd still be counseling people, listening to their problems. But, God willing, I would have had children. Would I now be proud of them, or would that have been a disaster? Although I never let them know it, sometimes the school children get on my nerves. Maybe I wouldn't have been a good father.* He suppressed a smile. *Was I any good at being a "father" to my flock?*

Father O'Malley blinked when he realized the deacon had finished reading the gospel. He rose for the Prayers of the Faithful; following them, he stepped over to the altar and recited the Mass prayers almost in a singsong fashion. The congregation stood and joined in when he reached the Lord's Prayer. At the

Sign of Peace, he looked out at the pews and waved to the O'Haras who always attended daily Mass, the general's wife who came alone most of the time, and to Sister Louise, now retired. He blinked when he spotted the young couple who'd just lost the month-old baby he'd baptized. They were sitting in a back pew on the side area. As they hugged each other, he could see the sadness in their eyes.

I'm glad I never had to suffer through losing a child, he consoled himself.

The Mass ended. After telling the congregation, "Go in peace to love and serve the Lord," he received help descending the steps. On the way down the aisle, he passed a lady he didn't recognize, but she looked familiar somehow. She followed him to the back of the church.

As soon as they reached the holy water fount, she touched his arm and motioned him over by the sacristy door.

"Father O'Malley," she said, "I guess you don't remember me. It's been many years, but I'm Susan Stein Lewis." She lowered her voice to a whisper. "But I bet you remember the night you kissed me goodbye and said you were going to the seminary."

Father O'Malley glanced in all directions. He hoped the parishioners passing by didn't hear her remark. "Oh, Susan. What a nice surprise. How has life treated you?" he asked, recalling what a tease she'd always been.

"I've had a very good life. My husband, John, is very successful. He's an engineer, retired now, so we moved back to my hometown. We have two children, the oldest, John Jr., is also an engineer. The younger one, Timothy," She chuckled and blinked, "well, he's almost middle-aged but still finding himself." She pulled out a picture of a handsome man with carrot red hair and a winning smile and held it up. Her voice lowered. "John doesn't know it but I named him for you."

She edged closer. "Look, Tim, er, Father, he's in jail on drug charges and burglary. I came to ask you to say some prayers for him." Her mouth twisted in a smug look that he remembered fondly. Then she added, "If things had been different, Timmy might have been your son," and Father Tim caught his breath.

He put his arm around her shoulder. *Oh, dear God, my memories are flooding back. No, I never forgot that last kiss. I think I loved her. My decision, was it right? Timmy? He's got red hair like mine was before it turned white. Would he have been different if I'd been his father?"* He blinked. *How am I going to handle this?*

He stiffened his body, stepped back, and held Susan at arm's length. "Since Timmy is your son, Susan," he said in a firm tone of voice, "I'm sure he's enough like you to overcome adversity. Give him a little time and keep praying for him and he'll be all right."

Father O'Malley steadied himself by leaning his back against the wall. "Suz," he used his pet name for her, "I'm convinced that you know the right things to tell Timmy to turn him around, back to God. Let go and let God take care of it." He nodded. "And I'll keep him in my prayers."

The tears in his former girlfriend's eyes melted his heart. He hoped he was telling her the truth. But it was time for dismissal. He looked at his watch. "I'm sorry, but I have to go. A baptism. Thank you for coming by." He squeezed her elbow. "Keep the faith." He didn't extend an invitation to come again.

It wasn't until Suz left that he realized how ludicrous his statement was—"Keep the faith." Suz was not Catholic; she was Jewish and deeply entrenched in her religion. He was also totally committed to his. That situation was a definite obstacle to happiness. Their marriage could have turned out to be a very shaky one.

Walking back to the rectory, Father O'Malley raised his eyes to the sky. *So, the baptism's not until this afternoon, but I had to have an excuse to leave, Lord, before I got in some real trouble. Ah, age doesn't end feelings. Suz was quite a looker and she's still a charmer—and a tease.*

Looking back at the church, the priest made the Sign of the Cross. People often told him secrets, some of which they harbored all their lives and he was bound by the seal of the confessional never to reveal them. Father O'Malley bit the corner of his lip. *How ironic nobody knows I have my own secret.* Realizing that his calling was to listen to parishioners' secrets rather than discuss his own, he sighed. The power to give them absolution for their sins was a tremendous responsibility, one he was willing to take. *I may be an old man, but I learned something from that encounter with my old girlfriend: the church is my home; I made the right decision.*

LAUGHING JESUS

A priest kept a picture
on her desk,
"The Laughing Jesus."

And he was, looked
like he had sense of humor,
needed one

in a world of poor Jews,
tax collectors,
Roman soldiers,

Pharisees.
But most who stepped
into her office

were offended,
even pissed off,
wanted, demanded

a dark Jesus,
a man of sorrows
who suffered only for them.

LOU ELLA HICKMAN, I.W.B.S.

THE SECRET OF THE COIN: PRAYER
AFTER THE 2016 ELECTION

i

how shall we pick up the stars
that have fallen from the sky
i, for one, will fling myself into that emptied darkness
after i gather them into my embrace that stretches
my arms wide
then in the beating of my heart's night
i will know the throbs of true love's pain

ii

here i am   sitting shiva
my nine days have just begun
my mourning
for the forest fire losses no one sees
the smoke becoming stale
still heavy among the blackened trees called souls
i watch   i wait   sitting among the scorched silences
that also sit behind the eyes that will not weep
                        and those who will sorrow themselves blind

Philip Martin

Tohu wa Bohu

The priest with the chalky eyes snapped the wafer into Charlie's hand only after the boy said, "Amen." It had been a few tense seconds. The priest had bent low to offer him the Body of Christ but Charlie leaned sideways like a curved pine to inspect the painting above the tabernacle. It caught his eye not only because it was new but also because he had seen it before, the hand of God with its index finger pointing and nearly touching the tip of another. Like a kindergartener's valentine it stood for something beautiful but would not hold to the scrutiny of an art critic. "The Body of Christ," the priest said again with emphasis on the nouns.

Amen.

Whenever Charlie slipped the host into his mouth, he had the sense that it ought to be chewed differently, like licking and sealing an envelope without staining the paper or creasing the fold. His mother chewed dinner like that on days when she would kick off her shoes at the door and, like instinct, raise her outstretched arm to the top shelf where the wine glasses did not have the chance to gather much dust. The only other body that Charlie had bitten into was his sister's, which cost him a week of cartoons. He put up a fight. If he was that desperate to watch television, his father told him in the garage, then he could sit in his mother's lap and learn something about real life from the news because the secondhand school that the city was funneling him into next year would not be teaching him. If Claver Middle lived up to its reputation, then the only thing he'd be learning there was how to speak Spanish.

When his mother brought him and his sister to Mass, they sat in the back pew to the priest's right when he was facing the people. Charlie preferred these seats to his father's favorite row in the middle of the church because he heard the priest say once that God in the end consigned the good kinds of people and animals to his right and the bad to his left. Whenever churchgoers came in late out of the heat and through the side door you could also be the first to look at them without their seeing you if your eyes were quick enough. Charlie had learned to look at people from his mother. From what would be whispered to him throughout Mass the boy often wondered why the priest did not mandate more of the sinners to sit at his left.

Minutes before falling in line with the march of communicants, as the altar bells chimed and Charlie shifted his weight from one knee to the next, his mother curled around the neck of his sister. She put her dry lips to his small ear.

"Six rows up, the man in the hideous grey suit. He's the councilman who voted to redraw the map."

Charlie studied the back of his head and tried to figure out how a man could redraw a map. Charlie pictured him as a much larger person with a bag of giant tools that could widen rivers and pull mountains from valleys. Whatever it was that the man could do, Charlie knew that it would cause him to go to a different school when August came. Something in him was excited about the change until he saw his mother's tears. This man hurt people with his maps.

Charlie let the wafer rest on his tongue as he walked step for step behind his mother as close to her as he could without clipping her heels. They skipped the chalice. A brief flash of light shot into the church as the mapmaker exited through one of the double doors behind the altar. Like a whip Charlie's mother grabbed his hand and yanked him through the side exit as his sister obediently followed. Almost like thieves, the three of them blazed a shortcut behind the shrubbery on the side of the church. Charlie's palm slipped from the grip of his mother, who like a predator rushed from the bushes and scurried into the parking lot where she and the mapmaker began to argue.

His sister sat on the curb and Charlie joined her, and he soon was dropping pebbles onto passing ants like some kind of god. The pitch and volume of the voices in the parking lot intensified, even as the two of them distanced themselves further from the church one small step at a time. His mother, clearly echoing pieces of the mapmaker's explanation, shouted big words like "population" and "rezoning." She was good at making people feel guilty. Beyond those two, through the mirage of the melting concrete, a small child that Charlie figured to be about his age hurled a tennis ball onto the roof of the church hall and tried catching it behind his back. After five tries, he finally achieved the feat and seated himself beneath the shade of a nearby oak.

Crowds began to pour through the doors like a pipe that had sprung a leak. Lines formed for coffee and donuts around two tables under the shade of an area for picking up and dropping off in the rain. Children ran in circles with sticky fingers and grownups raised their voices to talk over one another as they cast quick glances at the exchange of words thirty yards distant. Families walked out of their way to avoid being in close proximity to the argument as they set out for their minivans and SUVs.

Charlie's mouth dried up. He needed fresh water, not orange juice, and as a fish swims upstream, he fought the crowds to reenter the church to sip from the water fountain at the back. What he found instead was the priest who, despite his failing knees, lay prostrate before the image. In the quiet his deep whispers carried like a gentle breeze. The boy, so as not to interrupt, slowly backed out and rejoined his sister on the curb.

A few minutes past the close of Mass a sizeable crowd still lingered, and it polished off the remaining refreshments. Without warning, there was a loud crack and the breaking of glass. Everyone turned to gape at the man and woman nearly at each other's throats in the parking lot, and Charlie and his sister jumped to their feet. All were expecting to see one or the other of the quarrelers lying on the ground and bleeding, but instead both Charlie's mother and the mapmaker were staring with looks of pure horror past the crowds and at the church doors. The noise like an earthquake roared a second time and all pivoted to witness a giant fist with an index finger outstretched and breaking through the double doors. The hand was too wide for the square frame, which began to bulge and crack open like the breaking of a violent dawn. Shards of wood shot into the air and the old bricks began to crumble like dry bread.

A mob of people, including the mother and the mapmaker, sprinted for the door. In this they were all united. Both men and women bundled on either side of the extended index finger and shoved with all their strength. High heel shoes were flung off and sport coats thrown to the ground, and although a few men tried to grip a knuckle with their arms like pliers, the sweat of their hands made it nearly impossible to do so. Fifteen seconds passed, then thirty, and neither party had advanced any further upon the other. Charlie could see the old priest through a window and made an oath that he would never tell his mother that the man of God was pushing the hand out with his cane and all the while whispering.

Like a fish pulled onto the dock, the hand began to shake side to side. The mob erupted like a volcano with a new surge of aggression and some men jumped off the backs of others and onto the top of the hand. A couple of them were thrust onto the concrete sidewalk and more than a few took blows to the head from a falling piece of brick or mortar.

Charlie and his sister were the only two children who had not been corralled by three of the women behind a far-off automobile. A gust of wind surged forth from behind them and ripped napkins from under paper cups. A handful of dust and leaves were spun into a small whirlwind, which passed between Charlie and the fist and turned him towards it. He gasped. He was being drawn into the middle of the mayhem and it was no longer his decision. A fisherman had hooked him and he took a step in the direction of the church. His sister snatched the back of his belt for a moment but let it go, most likely thinking that Charlie was going to retrieve their mother. Despite the mob of adults, a path lay open before him to the hand since no one dared to go near the dangerous tip of the pointed finger. It beckoned him. In anticipation of his mother questioning his approach, Charlie tried to think up a reason to draw near to such an unbridled force but none came to him. He was there, merely inches away, and in a strange embrace, he put one arm on top and one beneath in a hug of some kind and rested his head on the fingernail.

The finger withdrew itself from Charlie's grip and the multitude began to cheer. For a few, brief seconds it appeared as if they had succeeded in forcing the fist back into the church where it belonged. The men relaxed their grips and those women who had been striking it with the heel of a shoe took a deep breath. Then, a flash of lightning. The finger struck Charlie in the chest with a viper's speed and the boy was shot backwards like a rock from a slingshot. From the point of view of the gasping crowd this was an assault that could not go without further beating, but to Charlie it was the gentle kiss of his grandmother at the threshold of her home. Charlie's mother and a few other sweaty women converged on the boy lying prostrate on the asphalt.

The fist paused for a moment before sliding back into the hidden darkness of the church. The mapmaker and another man reached to close the doors, but upon seeing that they lay shattered on the ground and there was no frame to close them into, they stood guard until a pickup truck could be parked at the entrance as a barricade. Charlie was rolled over by the many hands, which then lifted his shirt and rubbed his rib cage to see if it was smashed to pieces. It was not, and Charlie rose to his feet.

The crowd took their time in departing the scene. Like a football team that has won a very close match they stood around and panted with their hands on their heads. Some seemed eager to relay an eyewitness account to the police or a news camera. One man winced when he stepped on a shard of brick in search of his shoes but laughed it off knowing that the worst was over. Others drifted from one person to the next, giving hugs and shaking hands, after all having found some common ground. Even Charlie's mother and the mapmaker momentarily embraced until like ships with snapped anchors they inevitably drifted once more into the rough waves of their worldly ideals, and the shouting match resumed.

Charlie did not share their relief. He wanted it back. It had met him, touched him, kissed him, befriended him. And then it left. Something was missing now, something that ought to be there. No, it was in him. On the tip of his tongue, at the front of his mind. Something. The finger had chosen him for a reason. He apart from all the others had beheld it behind the priest, who at this moment was weeping silently on the other side of a cracked window. He had been beckoned. Then it occurred to Charlie that the fist had not told him something, but rather had asked him something. The finger had planted in him a question, not an answer. There it was, springing up in his mind like the dawn and in only a few moments it sprouted and budded and bloomed. That is when Charlie, through a smile gave his answer with the strength and peace of one whole breath: "Yes."

The boy turned on his heels and walked away.

"Where are you going?" his sister yelled to him.

"Come and see," he called back as he crossed the parking lot. The heat was more than heat out there. It was feeling; it was noise, and its hum was enough to frighten away many of the adults from following him even if a part of them had wanted to. An ultimatum of his mother commanding that he return danced about him and remained with him as if it were an option. Charlie endured the sauna until he came to the shade of an oak tree where the humming and the glare and the demands came to an end.

"Hey, what's your name?" Charlie asked the boy with the ball.

"Miguel."

"I'm Charlie. Where are you from?"

"My family just moved here a year ago," the boy said as he ground his feet into the dirt.

"Where do you go to school?"

"Claver Middle," Miguel responded.

"Hey me too. Do you want to play wall ball? I used to play it at my old school all the time."

The boy looked up. He blinked and turned his eyes away as a subtle smile flashed across his face like a ripple on a glassy sea. "Yes, but I do not know how."

"I'll teach you," Charlie said. "Let's play!"

The boy with the ball tossed it to Charlie who flung it against the wall with enough speed to shatter a window. Charlie dropped the rebound and sprinted to the wall laughing as if the other knew the rules. It was a teaching moment.

NATHANIEL BLAESING

BUILDING A NEST

With mud to keep out the breeze, we made a home far from sounds, or predators. I chose the tree where you now sit, wove the space where you would first breathe, and the place where you could branch out.

How can I teach you the things I've learned without knowing a language you'll understand? What will be the substance of your first thought? To whom will you speak when you know the words? Where will they lead you next?

When will you be tall enough to spread your wings? Will you survive the fall to adolescence? Will you parent as I have, and will you need what I've tried so hard to teach you about our world?

When your egg began to hatch, and you emerged all fluff, no feathers, I didn't know how to begin. Everything happened so suddenly even though I was expecting. I don't know if you've learned the things I needed to tell you, but you've taught me what I've needed to know.

Now that you've learned to hunt and fish through many migrations of rebuilding our nests, I know it is time. For all I have taught you about the path I'd hoped to lead you on, you will make your own. And then, perhaps, I will realize it was me who was meant to learn all these years. You've known what to do inside all along. You may not feel ready, but it is in your nature.

VIVIAN SHIPLEY

AGAINST THAT NIGHT

A bitter edge has been added today. As a small boy,
Eric fought off going to sleep, never wanting
to say goodnight to me, smiling like Savin Rock's

lady in the glass case rocking in her orange and red
flowered dress. I was sure where fact and fiction met,
like hands pressed to a mirror, until confirmation class

became a dance my son did around Sunday morning
authority, until I got the church's call asking why he
had dropped out. Like juggling snowballs after they melt,

Eric's face stays with me. My son knows how to head
soccer balls, but not about the thrust of a tongue. When
some girl touches him, he will not think of my love,

my hands peeling potatoes. Will he shiver, shake off
water like our golden retriever does after climbing out
of High Lane Pond? Cupping car keys, nothing I can

mouth about speed, alcohol, Scott who died last fall
at sixteen will inflate a raft to keep him afloat. Lifting
slats of the blinds, I watch him back out the drive. I am

left with memory of sweeping blacktop to clear worms
lured by promise in spring rain. Pulled from sleep, I wait,
then palm the hall to Eric's room. Reaching out for

the light switch, I stop. A voice I do not recognize comes
from his bedroom and stubs the dark. Will he tell me if
the girl's hands pulled him down? Knowing just what

a mother can't ask her son, what he won't answer, I jerk
questions back. Edging corners, I crabwalk to bed, stalked
by her whisper shrilling like wings of a swan in the night.

Sylvia Plath Should Have Planted a Garden

Lemon day lilies open their lips at noon in the garden
of the Strawbery Bank Museum as if waiting to be
fed by Puritans who brought them to New Hampshire,
planted roads leading to Portsmouth. New Englanders
dug clumps to transplant. Impossible to erase, like

dandelion roots, orange field lilies bank interstates
in July but they are too common to invade this exotic
collection of plants, laid out as if quilted and edged into
blocks of English herbs. About to climb a widow's walk
that crowns the house owned by a sea captain, the lure

of an opium poppy's round pod, grayish green leaves
with white and purple flowers, draws me outside.
Volunteers have yanked out chickweed that does
a slow boil in cedar and bull thistle, already punk
with heads of seed, has been carted off for compost.

I almost see the captain returning after two years:
hands on hips, elbows bent outward, arms akimbo
like lamb's quarters. His wife's shoulders might be
bare as the iris tubers, her need strong enough to push
through winter into spring in spite of shovel after

shovel of dirt. Would she have known to collect yellow
brown juice of unripe poppy capsules to mix an opiate
to stop time, thought? Did she count out black seeds
like dropping pills to stop the unattended pain of giving
birth alone then burying a child born too many months

after her husband set sail? She had no woman doctor
to befriend her, to give alkaloids of morphine, codeine
or papaverine to produce sleep after performing
an abortion on Sunday so there would be nothing
recorded at the clinic for a passion that should have

been controlled. In the museum shop, I start to ask
if the captain gathered poppy seeds on a trip to China.
Selling note cards picturing Strawbery Bank Museum,

an old woman sits in a stiff cotton dress. I hadn't
smelled starch since I was little: the steam, my mother

testing the hot iron with her spittled finger, the hiss
that always startled her. Smell, evanescent as everything
we can't hold onto, pulls at my body, reminds me
of games I was good at playing: Statues, Red Light,
Jailhouse. I would freeze, not a finger moving, an eye

blinking, invisible and never caught. *May I help you?*
jerks me back. I ask to buy poppy seeds from her or
gather them from the garden but that is illegal. Pulling
a sweater over her name tag, the woman says she will
give away what she can't sell, send me some from out

of her sister's garden even though it will mean breaking
the law. No return address, an envelope arrives; I plant
seeds, careful to follow her directions and store what I
don't use in an unmarked spice jar. However small, these
illicit acts between women bind us together, keep us alive.

Maria Terrone

Afghan Shadows

At the fundraiser, the famous TV reporter
told us the woman's story:
it was forbidden to record
a female face, and so she interviewed her
in shadow, the woman's hands

doing most of the talking.
Newly widowed, the woman hoped to remain
nameless, but her unique wedding ring
gave her away. So they locked her
indoors, nailing wooden boards

across the windows, blocking even her shadow.
After cocktails and dinner,
the woman's teenage daughter stood before us.
All clinking and murmur stopped
in the glittering hall as she grasped

for the right words in a strange language
to pull herself up, as if from a pit.
My murdered father and *our prison*
were the first to prick me, leaving their small
but unmistakable entry wounds.

Her mother lives now behind the walls
of an Afghan women's refuge
where her body, moving in sunlight,
casts a shadow again, and her mind
is slowly leaving its shadows behind.

Ruth Kessler

Camouflage

Later, you will master the art of camouflage.

On the front porch you'll place pots of red geranium,
hope's climbing ivy, smiles.
To point the way to strangers,
you'll light up in your eyes
memories of passion, joy.

Let only precious few glimpse
in your basement the chests
of missed chances,
drawers filled with wounds and fears,
shelves stacked with disappointments, jars of tears.

Let no one have the key
to your secret garden,
with its shed of knives and tridents,
its path leading to the quicksand
patch, the black swamp.

Dear Dr. Freud

How arrogant, how fraudulent your claim
to have found the master key to
our psyche's secret clockwork,
to the heart's hermetic gates—
asserting we can know ourselves
and one another.

The endless caravan of your disciples presume it still,
proclaiming their authority and skill will lead
them to the source,
to find in its unfathomable depths
the sacred fountain
of the soul.

When all you did—
and all they manage still—is
like the archeologist, who
having excavated a fragile manuscript
or shard of clay,

at last is able
after much analysis and probing
to theorize causality,
corroborate a pattern,
decipher fragments of inscriptions.

The rest—
lacunas, endless speculations,
mystifying maze of guesswork,
concealing behind age-old layers
the elusive
owner.

POLYGRAPH

What are they sampling,
these slender antennae

whose clubbed tips
startle and drift

over paper tape?
Which truths

do they taste,
how many

evade
the thin dark

sap they weep?

Liz Dolan

Recollecting Ethel Rosenberg's Execution for the Crime of Giving Secrets to the Soviets, 1953

When young, Ethel's rabbi riddled her on the Talmud,
If a man is washed overboard with his wife and son,
and can save only one, whom should he save?
The wife, she is the tree, she will again bear fruit.
Minutes before her execution, in a green print dress
and prison slippers, hair cropped, her rabbi begs her
to confess, *Your husband is dead. Save yourself*
            for the sake of your children.
I have no names to give. I am innocent.
She kisses her prison matron on the cheek.
And leaves her two sons floating out to sea.

While we in school giggle, scramble under our desks,
heads tucked, knees bent like blue and white turtles
retreating into our shells,
                    waiting for the bomb to drop.
Is she the spy who brings us to our knees,
hangs dog tags about our skinny necks?
Doesn't she deserve the chair like Cagney,
whose squeals deafen me each night,
as he is dragged down Death Row in the Big House?
Then why do I pray this dowdy housewife,
drying the dishes in her floury apron in a kitchen
not far from my own, would repent,
would save herself from being fried,
                    would not orphan her young sons?
Maybe, already, I could smell something burning.

T.K. Thorne

A Dead Mockingbird

My Pa is dead.

They say he fell on his knife.
No.
That Boo boy kilt him.
The kids told it true.

My Pa is dead.

Tom Robinson's dead too,
shot dead.
His blood red as my geraniums
against the rotted fence.

But I couldn't get the smell of either off me.

I head to the woods,
to the cold creek.
To walk in, my clothes clinging like sin
and look up through the water,
drowning my eyes with stars.
They stare back like all those glances
that flitch flesh
when I pass.

There goes that girl, that Mayella,
their silent stares say.
She tried to seduce a Negro,
a dead Negro now,
but still.

"Rape," they declare
to each other.

They will never understand
the black, deep pit of my desiring—
my need
to have something 'cause I wanted it
'cause *I* said
I need.

It was always what Pa wanted.
What he said
he needed.

I was a worm squirming in the dark soil,
yanked out,
hooked,
fed
to the hungry fish.

My Pa is dead.

Tom Robinson's dead, the Negro
that I desired.
My world I shattered
into pieces.
Like the stars,
they stare back at me.

I won't be missed,
'cept maybe by my geraniums.

JOHN BLAIR

PERFECT FIFTY

The bus pulls into the New Orleans terminal, and I step out with the other travelers. A sign beside the row of ticket windows shows the date, big sliding plastic numbers. It strikes me suddenly that this day of all days is my birthday. Fifty years old. One perfect half-century. I try to think if I feel any different, and I think maybe I do, though not like I'd expect. The city rumbles with midnight traffic. I start to walk, and when the twenty minutes for the rest stop are over I'm still walking. I come to the river and above the levee I can see the lights of a tanker ship moving slowly, like something from another world cruising low in the night sky. I climb up the slope and stand looking out at the dark river. On the low batture, a small fire burns. I can see faces in the firelight and realize it's three kids, maybe fifteen or sixteen, drinking, passing a bottle around. Probably not locals, out in the open like this. Runaways. Travelers. Three to make an imperfect half-century. An almost. I squat in the grass and tap a cigarette out of my pack. I smoke and watch and imagine them each and lovingly dead. Murdered and sunk young and unknowing in the river. The kids don't care, or notice. The river hones itself against the rip-rap and passes indifferently by. One of the kids laughs, and the sound is like gravity, a pull made of longing that never stops. I grind out the butt, and stand up and walk away along the levee. When I look back, the fire is a spark almost hidden by the dark arc of the levee's shoulder. I blow a little kiss to that flicker of light. Wish all the lost children that don't know any better the temporary blessings of peace and safe passage, from waking to sleeping and back again. On and on until they reach whatever possible perfection that waits somewhere just for them.

ROY WHITE

THE CUP

I dip it in the stream
and feel as I drink
smooth enamel, soft gold,
the bumps of deep-red gems.
I think of its ancient maker, maybe
a captive like me, taken
and bound to his arcane craft.

In each night's pigsty
or wasted fen-fastness,
I hug it for warmth, I
a wolf-head, fair game for any man,
but not without treasure.

I saw the worm last night,
no moon, just a dragon-
shaped hole in the stars,
and later the angry glow
of distant flames. My own fire
I built without fear.

When I took it from the old hoard,
I thought, "Here is a token
to soothe the Master's rage, but knew
he'd only snatch it up
and shackle me for a thief.
No, it is my secret now,
as it was the dragon's.

The Master will not understand
what has angered the worm; well,
fuck him! And fuck you all, noble
loaf-guards with your stupid
mead-halls and your stupid names,

Prosperity Friend and He Who Takes
Advice from Elves.

If I manage to live a while
taking a lamb or chicken now
and then, you'll start calling me
the Aglæca; some nights
a frightened child will see a dark
shape drawn to the edge of the clearing
by the red gold of the bonfire.

Thomas DeConna

My Neighbor, Mr. Keats, Spring 1819

I am a dowager of sixty years:
slight, stooped, but sprightly in heart and mind.
In April I saw my next door neighbor,
Mr. Keats, emerge from a drear and dree
winter's slumber, not a physical sleep—
an emotional one that included
a younger brother's tubercular death
and a misconstrued Valentine's Day card.
My psyche bestows blame on Mr. Brown,
a proud, pompous man with a wanton eye.
The cunning manner with which he measures
Abigail, a new-hired Irish lass—
no good will come of their proximity.

But I turn to John Keats who paid visit,
asking for parchment, for he had used all
and was ill-prepared a venture to town.
True, he is small in stature, yet somehow
spans the room with a warm, manly presence
paired with a humble sensibility.
His speech alters from passionate to pale.
His eyes widen, sparkle, and absorb all.
He is as handsome as true happiness
and tells me he has been writing full sore.
I ask the matter of composition,
and he replies, "Poetry." Ah, indeed,
he portrays the part like etchings on urns.
Of three visitors he tells me: "Poesy,
Ambition, and Love." What then should I glean
from his visions of unreflecting love?
Yet I persuade my young Keats to take tea
and weekly visit me, a widow of
meager means that a pot of basil might
hold or a purse fill with nightingales' songs.

So, every seventh day he sojourns
as we sip tea and the poet reveals
melancholy moods and indolent sighs.

The weather is especially vibrant
as weeks pass and May blooms with violets,
hawthorn, eglantine, and fruit trees wild.
Keats visits and shares his aching sorrows
and fears that he may cease to be before
reaping the boundless harvest within him.
He tells me of another brother who
emigrated to America, lost
all assets, yet supports wife and child.
It so upsets my Endymion friend,
especially when George returned, asking,
shamelessly, for pounds not to be repaid.
With scant funds about him, Mr. Keats
paid the sought sovereigns, but promised me
he would never rise from cool-bedded grass,
and cares would vanish like an idle sprite.

At Wentworth Place, a family now shares
the house with Mr. Brown and Mr. Keats:
Mrs. Brawne, a widow, too, with three fair
children. Fanny is eighteen and eager
to touch the mortal world. Fanny merges all
John's fears and hopes in a feminine frame.
I judge her to be a flirty minx-girl,
but Mr. Keats, smitten, grows to adore
her robin's egg eyes and magic-chance cheeks,
her fairy-kissed brow, soft voice, and warm lips
that dazzle. 'Tis well enough, yet she aims
towards something more. Love deepens like shadows,
compassion turns steadfast, bright as a star,
and love blooms like the dewy musk-rose that
endows each sense with ripeness and fire.

As a light autumn wind might live or die,
Keats changes chameleon-like from despair
to ease wherewith, he claims, a negative
capability, which I cannot seize.
I see him with writing tablet softly
steal out of doors and set a chair to sit.
Fair youth, beneath a plum tree, composes

his verse while Fanny in homespun splendor,
like a muse, intuits to come or go.
In silence she walks with aurorean
love and spies his clandestine creation.
Yet Miss Brawne is the heat that inspires
this dreaming sun, this tender-taken star.

More tea and time and troubled spirits; John
tells me of a sister he seldom sees
and thinks himself her only protector.
Fanny wears a gold ring with almandine,
yet their courtship is silent as a town
deserted. Keats lacks all means, and Fanny's
without parental approval. And worse,
John's inner conflict between desires:
love of writing and of being in love.

He *must* have money; he *must* write without
distraction warming his veins. Brown offers
a plan: to collaborate on a play
steeped in history. To leave Wentworth Place
for the summer and live with library
at hand. I suggest Winchester and wish
I were a patron to Hyperion
and fret that I shall never see my friend
in such health and beauty again; in truth,
I fear he shall pass before me and not

live to trace cloudy symbols or bright shades.
I swear that heaven is a weeping cloud;
joy turns to hemlock and begs me to drink.
Shall his name be writ on shifting water?
Will the enchanted spring ever return?
Will beauty and love keep their lustrous eyes
tomorrow, or is all forlorn and pale?
What cheats my hope so well? Adieu, adieu:
blessed one, indolence, melancholy,
Grecian urns, and inciting nightingales.

LAURENCE SNYDAL

BONING A PORK LOIN

Along the line of bone I shook
And shivered, dug inside, unseen,
Unseamed this lump of flesh, this lean
Loin lying open like a book.
I read red rooted out, alone.
I eased my narrow edge between
Meat and its matrix, slicing clean
Through thrip and thread to cold bare bone.
I drew the cunning edge to free
The slatted ribs, the gristled clot,
The essence of this flesh, unknot
The puzzle in its heart and see
An end to secrets. Here I laid
All secrets open with my blade.

JANE ST. CLAIR

THE GERBER SECRET

I can understand on some level when a child does not have enough to eat, she will be left with a terrible scar, perhaps one that reaches deep into her soul. Perhaps if she is lucky, growing up hungry will just make her weird. In my mother's case, whatever happened to her in the 1930s left her so anxious and scarred that she was afraid to leave the food in her kitchen. Flanked by a full Frigidaire and a Whirlpool stove covered with boiling stockpots, she would stand at her Formica countertop, chopping and mincing while listening to "The True Adventures of Helen Trent" on the radio. Helen Trent was a woman who did more with her life than chop and mince, and her adventures supplied my mother with the fantasy of the world she lived only to avoid.

My mother felt safe only when she was near food. She bought enormous amounts of food and justified that strategy by economies of scale. There was half a cow in her deep freezer, several gallons of ice cream, and bag after bag of hard, green, yellow and red frozen hard vegetable jewels that she had chopped and minced herself. She kept jars and jars of pasta, except we called it macaroni, and troves the size of pirates' treasure chests of flour, sugar, coffee and beans. She bought in fifty-pound measures for the two of us. She kept a walk-in pantry as big as most people's living rooms and that she filled with Mason jars of food she canned herself.

Mother always kept a Victory Garden and would never live where you could not have one. When the next Depression came with its accompanying climate change and Dust Bowl, she and I would be saved by raising our own food. Mother believed that The Government would allow us to keep chickens, goats, and perhaps even a small cow once the Depression came again. In times like that, The Government made allowances with what you could do with your land. Like Scarlet O'Hara, we could get by if Mother could hold on to Tara. *Land, Land, Land!*—and she'd never go hungry again.

Mother invested only in gold and never bought anything on credit. She took pride in how she could stretch a dollar and make do with what others threw out, and she always shopped at thrift stores.

Perfectly Good was Mother's mantra. Perfectly Good curtains and Perfectly Good rugs. From time to time, I would catch Mother picking up some Perfectly Good thing off the street—a rain hat, a ballpoint pen, even shoes—Perfectly Good shoes with a lot of wear left in them. During the Depression, she had to take turns going to school with her two sisters because they shared a pair of shoes.

The corollary of the doctrine of Perfectly Good is Just as Good. The ten-year-old blouse from the thrift store is Just as Good as the Bobbie Brooks sailor blouse in style right now. The ugly brown oxfords from Sears are Just as Good as the Buster Browns advertised on television, even though they do not have a picture of Buster Brown and his dog Sandy inside them. No one wears pictures anyway. Mother's sponge cake cut into squares is Just as Good as Twinkies. You don't eat packaging.

Though we lived on what other people threw out, we ourselves never threw anything out. We kept old string and twined it into a large ball. We used birthday and Christmas paper from one year to the next, and we handed down hand-me-downs. Mother had drawers full of cloth scraps, ribbons, buttons, small bits of paper, pencil stubs, rubber bands, artificial flowers, screws, pins *ad infinitum*. Things ordinary people chunk away into just one junk drawer, we categorized and stored twelve junk drawers for the next real national emergency.

Mother's philosophy—the philosophy of the poor—was that something is always better than nothing. To this day when I participate in toy or clothing drives for the poor, it bothers me when organizers insist that every donation must be new. It's as if the organizers don't understand the philosophy of poverty: something is always better than nothing and a used toy is better than no Santa at all.

Another rule of the poor is that if something eats, it must prove itself worthy its food. Mother practiced that rule. Once I picked up a stray dog that was part-poodle: the graven image of dogs owned by stars like Bardot and Mansfield. The dog had winning ways: she was a born suck-up and even my mother fell for her. We named her Oo-La-La. My mother justified the cost of the dog's food because she provided the service of barking at strangers, warning us Just in Case we were internally attacked. Eventually my mother found another use for the dog by collecting the hair she shed and using it as pillow stuffing. If there was not enough dog hair, she would add lint from the dryer.

I married young and left Mother living alone for years. This was better for her because she could gain even more control over her expenses. She only had to heat one room in the winter—the kitchen—and she would heat with her stove instead of her furnace. She sent my children five dollar checks on their birthdays and Christmas, wrapping each check in a bit of paper so as to save money on cards. Her diet grew more bizarre. She still bought food in bulk and ate the same thing for days on end, as if she were a lion with a big carcass. Yet in her own way, my mother was happy. She had complete control over everything, perhaps even the terrible events of her childhood.

Mother was only fifty years old when she got cancer, and her first reaction to her diagnosis was to read over her insurance policies. She wanted to be sick at home and on the cheap. When she was dying, I moved back home.

The situation was so depressing to me that I consulted a psychic. I went into her dark strange little house with its beaded curtains at the windows and its tables that move by themselves and its gaudy crystals dingling everywhere.

"Your mother?" she said as I walked into her reading room.

I nodded, too overcome by emotion to speak. I sat across from her at the moving table as she went into a trance and told me things I did not want to hear.

"What your mother tried to control all her life," she said, "is now taking over her body. Growing and multiplying and taking over her organs and pushing themselves into her bodily spaces."

At that time my mother had so many tumors that many of them were visible on the outside. In particular, there was one big round gray mass on her throat. Her nurse told me that for every tumor I could see on the outside, there were at least ten on the inside. Now I had the awful image of uncontrolled, unrelenting growth from this bizarre psychic.

"You need to tell your mother to let go of her past," she said. "Her sick is about garbage accumulating and growing and taking over. Tell her to throw out the garbage."

I left as soon as I could because the woman was weirding me out. Not only had she used a medieval phrase, "her sick," but she looked like a medieval witch.

The first thing I did when I got home was to collect all the dog-hair pillows in the house and pile them up in the living room. Then I tore off all the stiff and yellowing plastic seat covers that had protected our furniture for decades and decades. I ripped and shredded them off every sofa and chair in the house and piled them up in the living room.

Then I attacked the kitchen. Half of Mother's food was spoiled. Her flour bin was full of little yellow worms. I knew my mother felt that such flour was Perfectly Good to use as long as she cooked it very hard. But that day I threw the wormy flour out. I threw out frozen foods that had dates more than ten years old. I threw out Mason jars of tomatoes and peaches and green beans that no one would ever want or need or use.

I went through the drawers and threw out ribbons, buttons and scraps of cloth. I found old dresses from the 1930s so frayed that the wool in them crumbled when I touched them. I took pair after pair of Perfectly Good shoes in sizes no one could wear and piled them up in the living room, now heaped with garbage as big as a freight car. On some level I believed that if I threw out all the things Mother had accumulated, I could cure her.

That night a water pipe mysteriously broke open and water gushed out, covering the floors like an undiscovered lake and seeping out doors and into the neighbor's yards. Our house was giving the gift of water, sweet nutrients flowing out of our house and into someone else's. For the first time in thirty years everything flowed and flowed and we were giving something away.

That same night my mother pulled me to her bedside and she told me the secret of her life. She was unaware of the garbage heap in the living room and that water was flooding our floors even as her secret flowed out of her, a secret that shocked me to the ground of my being.

The story she told was this. After my father was killed in the war, she had taken his entire life insurance policy of $25,000 and invested it in manufactured baby food. She figured that when the boys came home from the war, they would want home, hearth and babies. She banked on the premise that all the women waiting for them would want to get pregnant right away.

"I thought people would be stupid enough to believe that this food is better than mother's milk," she told me. "I figured they would all buy it."

With what little strength my mother had left in her body, she directed me to go into her closet and retrieve a metal strongbox with her stocks in it.

"I didn't think you would ever gamble," I said as I brought the box to her.

"I never gamble," she said. "This was a sure thing. I knew women would buy this food. They would want to produce the Master Race with all these fancy vitamins and minerals. How do you think the Germans fell for Hitler? It was our times. I figured the same would happen here. They would believe in this magic food and not nurse their babies. This was food they could control themselves."

The iron box had papers carefully filed in brown legal folders and envelopes. When I found her secret stock certificates, I saw that she had been right about the baby food. She had doubled and tripled her money many times over—time and time again. All the years I was growing up in poverty, my mother had been a very rich woman.

I had hoped to cure my mother, but her tumors did not fade away. They kept multiplying as ugly gray lumps under her flesh, an army of biological invaders defeating her from within. She died in my arms a few days later.

My mother never wasted anything. My mother wasted everything. My mother died a rich woman. My mother died a poor woman.

RODNEY TORRESON

THE LOCKED ROOM

Even as the grand old man received kin
near his recliner in the living room,
his shiny grace nearly absolved him
of the locked room, with shushing always
winning out against any rustlings
regarding the room that had grown like a tumor
since a padlock first took stock of it,
a room no one—save him—stepped a foot in,
while Great Grandma, locked
inside her skin, sat in her chair
on a soft cushion of sadness,
eyeing the key in the hollow of his left ankle,
outlined in socks he was knee-deep in
regardless of the weather.

At gatherings, the fuss with folding chairs
not finding us a place for us children to perch,
we'd be politely pushed into
the bathroom adjacent the locked room,
where we'd squat inside
the claw-footed tub or outside the rim
on which we'd balance our paper plates,
once in a while one of us getting up
to rattle the lock—quieting
 the buzzing inside us.

After his tractor tipped on him
for maybe living on the steep
side of a hill, and before I'd learned
that everyone has a locked room,
my great uncle opened the room,
and little he could say satisfied kin,
only that fifty years of shirts and ties
were piled to the ceiling

from a half century of birthdays
and holidays, shirts pinned like butterflies—
that never fit any of his lives.

There was no mention of Great Grandma's sister,
who folks half expected never died,
but was alive inside the locked room—
the sister he left Great Grandma at home for
on fishing trips up to Minnesota,
and when Great Grandma died—
it was the same day that Kennedy was killed,
his death causing her
to be overlooked yet again,
her dying just a matter of settling
deeper into one of her sighs.

AGE 9, DRESSED FOR SUNDAY SCHOOL
BUT FOR MY BLACK BOWTIE

kept in my parents' room
in a high side drawer
of their mahogany dresser,
I'd snare it by its bat-wing, aflutter
as I'd mount it onto my collar.

But one Sunday, thrusting further,
my palm caught on
what it read as a pack of cards.
and soon it fluttered like the bowtie,
as if my trembling hand aimed
to clamp it to skin,

for instantly my eyes were born
to desires I could not unlearn:
wanton eyes and demure smiles,
and to my horrid fascination
fleshly mounds with bigger, wider,
even lovelier eyes
that sized me up
by the lump in my throat,
which I swallowed,

only later to sweat out my sin,
then weeks of creeping back
toward the dresser,
where I abhorred the tie
for having to brush my hand past it
even on days it didn't
hang beneath my chin.

And, finally, I could take it no longer,
and, grasping the pack,
my hands stammered, "Why? Why?"
and my mother, startled,
threw her arms up and screamed
that the cards meant
nothing to her and my father.

"The low prize in cards, that's all!"

Out near the grove
to a brooding bonfire
I followed her,
watched her hurl the cards
into the wind,
which shuffled them into the flames.

And for months, I saw
her burning stare drawing me in
again and again,
a small boy
caught in the ashes of men.

KEVIN STEIN

DISCIPLES

When I turn to answer the dingaling,
my giddy mother skitters onto Fifth Street
to hitch a ride home *from* home, raising
in place of thumb a B&W photo of herself
at thirty-one, slim waist and bouffant.
What's left of her memory bank
writes bad checks as we plunk curbed
by horns and assorted Spanglish curses.
Settle down, dear reader—by dingaling
I mean my phone not her. We make more
sense not making sense so just stop trying
sang Talking Heads after Reagan got
elected despite CNN's bevy of talking heads,
my ringtone tune prescient if ironic.
In Alzheimer's kitchen she finger-shushes
so we listen to her coffee maker natter
Platte Deutsche, the toaster French,
all the spoons Russian dolls nestling faces
swallowed by black lacquer of absence.
Father, daughter, lost son. *Qu'est-ce que c'est?*
Listen, what's it to you if I hear those gadgets
squabble as her staticky fluorescent clicks off.
Who am I subverting but myself?
This nod I'll make to love and theft,
to the mind as body's high priest, or
its punch drunk acolyte—one always
on knee before the other's vacant chalice.

Audio Visual

Night's black crepe inked our anniversary boudoir video. Sure this sounds French but isn't creepy, itself a non-cognate of *crepe* in the fashion skin says less about flesh than what's inside yearning muchly to be out, moth at August's window screen. The word *muchly* I wish I'd made-up but verily it doth sound twelfth-century comely in ways "pulchritude" can't despite its pure Latin root. A pulchritudinous moth conjures huge and possibly toothed even though night yearns to swallow it, swallow itself conjuring Emerson on the _ _ _ _ _bed he'd forgotten half the word for, language a fossil reinterred as he was about to go out and into. Hear it? Knock-knock our marriage bed breaking on through to the *other* other side. Knock-knock the son awakened by our moving into and out of ourselves, then the plastic water cup and back-to-sleep-story cobbled between sobs. We made that, and him, as we were made by our parents' little bed-deaths before their last. Knock-knock began the world's first password. What's yours? *Shhhh.* We're the only two who'll know. Mine's not her maiden name or *pulchritude007*. Relax, it's all shadow anyway. Come in. Our video's ruffled-crepe-eclipse shows only where we were not—and in our bodies' absence where we'd gone off to, gotten off on, poof. The password? *we'reAllGoners.* Alas and rejoice.

To Rothko

"The people who weep before my pictures are having the same religious experience I had when I painted them."

-Mark Rothko

I've never stood before one of yours and wept—
unless you count this digitized "Orange, Red, Yellow"
projected on my Samsung 55" HD flat screen,
and really I don't so much sob as trampoline
in the presence of art. My boing-boinging
Walter Benjamin dismisses as toeing
the aesthetic ladder's low rung. Heehaw!
It's no secret I'm a rube. I'm the tipsy
south end of a north-going Angel of History.
No joke, laughter's always part moan.
Once heard, you'll never miss its mixed
bliss-and-sadness guffaw, dogma of wing
and root. If Joan of Arc burned for hers,
convicted of convictions, my Moan of Art
stakes the bad-pun rung of art's stepladder
I climbed in painterly thrall to brush
this poem in shades of brown: its homely
siding, gutters, steps, assorted window sashes.
It's the prairie's chocolate Chartres,
Easter Bunny cathedral in festive grass,
accented with *Candle*-scented candles.
Rothko, you're inside it now, neither of us
weeping, our less-noble Chernobyls
abandoned like dirty shoes outside the door
opened with whoosh of burning bush.

Repackaging Poems

These poems, like several other recent pieces, were originally written on postcards exchanged with poet Dean Young. Our common goal is to audition alternate means of writing and receiving poems—and to make that writing equal modes of discovery and play. On my end, I fashion oversized 6" x 11" postcard poems out of the paperboard boxes of common household items such as Wheaties cereal, Kashee cookies, and PBR 12-packs. I then handwrite each postcard poem and send it off via snail mail with a first-class stamp.

The process offers several surprising allures. One is the notion of writing in space circumscribed by the postcard's physical dimensions. One writes small and writes fast, exhilarated both by open possibility and by its inevitable constraint. As space gradually diminishes, the physical landscape under one's hand accentuates the redemptive intangibles of the writing experience one can't see.

The choice of these poems' graphical medium(s) also provides unexpected pleasures. Selecting, say, the familiar red, white, and blue of PBR packaging carries implications beyond my original intention simply to play with what I had at hand at home. One side's logo (should it be considered the back or the front?) asserts communal associations that the postcard's hyper-personalized flip-side poem disrupts via its handwritten scrawl. One side speaks to mass-market production and the other to art as individual act of making.

What's curious is how the commercial package has been physically as well as ideationally scissored open. It is, if you will, repackaged so that anti-commodity art can be inserted. In the process both items are remade and sweetly problematized. Think of how Walter Benjamin's magisterial "The Work of Art in an Age of Mechanical Reproduction" decries the diminished value of the mass-produced aesthetic object compared to the thing made singly by hand and head. Here, the solitary poem-as-art pairs, or perhaps wrestles, with mass-market packaging.

Crafted of these dissimilar entities, the postcard poem amounts to a one-off creation, an original fashioned once and only. The postcard poem, unlike the consumer item whose package it now shares thus reinterprets, is not meant for mass production or large-scale consumption. It enacts the poetry of a moment—composed of self and other, private intuition and shared culture.

As poet and scholar, I admit it's tempting to proclaim the repackaging motif of these postcard poems resulted from deep philosophical forethought. Alas, no. I've come to understand this notion only after months engaged in the muddled process of making. Still, I am even more gratified by the lucky wisdom of my random choices, itself a lesson in trusting one's foggiest aesthetic intuitions.

It turns out, you see, that both sides of these postcards—for instance, chocolate chip cookie and handwritten poem—feature items that give pleasure and value only when consumed. Many would suggest the cookie is cookie only when eaten, and the poem a poem only when read. After all, the gift of making things achieves its full measure when shared with others.

Jami Buck

Forgiving Daddy

In 1963, during my fifth year, we began a family tradition: brunch at the Broadwater Hotel. One Sunday a month, Mama and Daddy left the old wood-paneled station wagon in the driveway and put my brother and me in the backseat of our black Thunderbird. Dressed in a fine suit, Daddy smoked a cigar while driving. Mama, who was happy to be dressed up and heading toward entertainment, radiated contentment, while my brother, Chip, and I spent most of the ride defending our halves of the white leather backseat as we escaped the drab shipyard town of Pascagoula.

Daddy owned a business machine and office supply store. I couldn't imagine him working for anyone else. He always had to be in control of everything around him. So, he met with clients from New Orleans to Mobile, and made sure the repair guys in the shop at the supply store were working to service the machines of the day. Mama did the bookkeeping from the laundry room/office she'd created at home, and developed a working relationship with the secretary at the store. I grew up around classic typewriters and the smell of machine oil wafting through the door to the repair shop. In the store I had access to all the paper and writing instruments a creative girl could want. I did have to be careful about disturbing Daddy at work. If no one else was there he might make my brother and me scrub the floors. Sometimes he'd stand over us and yell for no reason we could tell.

Daddy was often a tyrant at home. The family could never relax when he was there. He and Mama had noisy fights that only grew worse as Chip and I grew older. And Daddy could ruin a vacation with his yelling and carrying on before we even got out of town. But on these days, as we headed for long drives on Biloxi Beach, he was as calm and mild-mannered as I ever saw him.

The Broadwater Hotel, with its pink dining room, modern and elegant, sat at the edge of the Gulf of Mexico. Walking into the cavernous Royal Terrace, I felt a sense of peace. The room was a warm shade of pink. As a child, I thought of it as "the pink dining room." It reflected the light from the swimming pool beyond. Watery shadows danced on the walls as Gulf breezes blew in from the beach. White sheer curtains, as high as the twenty-foot ceilings, billowed and swayed in the breeze. On a small stage at the corner of the dance floor, three old men in suits played a Bossa nova. Women wore dresses and high heels, some with hats, a few with netting.

Mama had two netted hats. When she removed them from their special striped boxes, she allowed me to try them on. She talked about the fun she'd had dancing to the big band music of the 1940s. She still had several pretty dresses she'd worn. My favorite was a strapless aubergine silk taffeta with crinoline under a full skirt and a bolero jacket. I wore it to costume parties until my mid-twenties. Mama's top dresser drawer was a treasure trove of costume jewelry from the 40s and 50s. I loved lying on her bed, my chin resting in my hands, feet in the air, talking with her and watching as she dressed in the lady-like layers of the day. Her undergarments included silk stockings and a garter belt. The small latch that held the stockings in place fascinated me, and I couldn't wait to be old enough to fasten my own pair. Mama enjoyed nothing more than dressing in a classic pencil skirt with a matching jacket, and enjoying beautiful surroundings. I loved being with her anytime, but mornings in her room—the smell of her perfume, all the little treasures, her happy mood—filled me with anticipation, especially when preparing for our Sunday brunches at the Broadwater.

The tables in the pink dining room were covered in white tablecloths, white china, and silver place settings, with pink cloth napkins to match the color of the walls. In the center of each table sat a tiny vase holding pink carnations. There were sparkling champagne glasses that were so shallow, I wondered how the grownups kept the liquid inside. Mama took off her gloves and placed them on her small beige handbag. She wore her pastel green suit with beige shoes to match her bag.

A bounty of fresh Gulf seafood, plus every breakfast food imaginable, was on the menu. We dined on shrimp, oysters, and eggs Benedict. There were hash browns, pancakes and waffles, crawfish etouffee, and all types of bread, including my favorite, brioche. It was a feast of traditional American breakfast fare with a smattering of Louisiana French cuisine.

At our table, my little brother squirmed in his suit and wiped his mouth on his sleeve. As Mother reached toward him to clean him up, I knew she was the most beautiful woman in the room. On the dance floor, couples swayed to the lively piano, double bass, and soft drums of the band. The music made my feet swing back and forth. I looked down at my black patent leather shoes and wondered when my feet would finally touch the floor. Daddy's hand appeared in front of me. I looked up at his face—his jet black hair glossy and neatly combed. His suit was royal blue, and he wore a crisp white dress shirt and skinny black tie with a favorite silver tie clip. With a wry smile he said, "My dear, would you like this dance?" I'd never danced with another person before, only my giant, stuffed panda. All those grown-ups moving around on the parquet floor seemed to know something I couldn't. Before I could protest, Daddy was standing in front of me, showing me how to put my feet on top of his. I couldn't believe he would let me stand on his nice shoes—this could create a terrible bout of yelling at home. I did as he said and we took off, swirling to the music, the sunlit room moving around me at almost dizzying speed. I threw my head back and laughed with delight. As we sailed past our table, Mama smiled, and Chip looked content.

I wish those days, that feeling of family, could've lasted forever, but at the age of twelve, I begged my mother to divorce Daddy. His alcoholism and mood swings had taken a terrible toll on each of us. No one in the house felt safe. Mama had been sleeping with me for two years. One morning, my daddy, who'd shown me his love of music and dance, who'd taken my brother and me to a tiny oyster house and had the owner hide Mama's old pearls in our oysters, began banging and yelling for Mama to open my bedroom door. When she didn't open it, he broke it down. It fell on my bed, almost hitting my leg. He stood there and screamed for what seemed an eternity. When Mama didn't respond, he spat on her. Much of it landed on me. Then he turned and stormed out of the house. My mother lay there, shaking and crying silently. I told her we couldn't go on with Daddy in the house. The next day, she called my sister, Leah, to ask if she'd come from Atlanta to be with her as she began divorce proceedings. Mama finally managed to protect us from Daddy's behavior. Yet even my sister didn't know how bad things had been at home. It was a secret known only to my mother, my brother, and the father I thought I no longer loved.

Without Mama in his life, Daddy declined. His business suffered. Instead of having coffee with other businessmen around town, he was seen out at night, drinking in local bars. It became clear to me as I grew older that Mother had been his confidence.

I didn't see my father much after the divorce. Because he was bitter toward Mama, I avoided him. Pascagoula is a small town, so I knew what was happening in his life. He descended into alcoholism, and his health deteriorated. He spent his final years living in a tiny apartment he'd built behind the business.

The last time I saw Daddy he was seventy-two years old and in the hospital on his death bed. This man, who photographed the beauty of Europe, who introduced us to music of Herb Albert and swam with my brother and me in the clear springs of Florida could no longer move or speak. His manicured feet were now a mass of gnarled bone and limp digits. I lifted the white sheet that covered his body and found his hand. It was also ravaged from arthritis. There were no bones. As I slipped my hand under his, I could feel his soft, rubbery fingers limp against mine. His eyes responded to my touch. He knew it was me, and he began to cry. A flood of emotion flowed out of me. I told him I wished we'd had a happy relationship. I told him I knew he loved me, even though his love was often hidden behind so much pain and anger. It was the closure I needed, and if he heard all I told him, I have to believe it helped him, too.

In 2005, the Broadwater Hotel and my beloved pink dining room succumbed to Hurricane Katrina's thirty-six foot tidal wave. The hotel lay in ruins, as did so many things from those early days of my life.

I wonder if my father thought of those days in the pink dining room. Did he remember my pretty dress, the weight of my small body as he lifted me onto his black leather shoes, the music playing as we whirled around the dance floor? When I think of those days at the Broadwater, I remember most being close to Daddy and feeling safe and loved. The smell of his cologne, mixed with a hint of his favorite Cuban cigars—the way he reached around the table to clink our glasses and toast the day with each of us. As we left the dining room, I would reach out and put my hand in his. He would squeeze my hand just a little, and I knew he loved me.

BENJAMIN MUELLER

GRAVEL

We didn't know
the word injustice
when we gathered

around to watch,
but we knew it was
fucked up the way

the gravel skidded
between the parked cars
at the fieldhouse,

the unlooked for
violence that ended
face down in the rocks.

Fist upon fist
pounding down. We
knew it was bad,

but we figured it
would be stopped
or punished the way

we were taught.
We didn't think
the football captain

would just peel out,
windows down, music
screaming—dust

parching our wordless
tongues, leaving us
wondering how we

should exit this scene
with Adam lying there,
gravel in his cheek

and forehead. And
on Monday, the hallways
filled with the same

clutter and cast as all
Mondays, jockeying
our way to classes.

Except Adam passing
through—pocked scabs,
gravel still buried

in his face. While
we swallow those
hard little stones

sticking in our throats
assuring ourselves that
one day, one day.

THE FELLOWSHIP OF CICADAS, MONTGOMERY COUNTY, 2011

Driving at dusk
through the starlit township
closeted with trees, I heard
the singing of cicadas

Invisible worshippers
what primeval instruments
keen and praise, take this
dying day to church

I am crossing through now
just passing through American
flags and fences picket
the civil rights of twilights

But what calm here
what immaculate houses
suburbia like in storybooks
I read long ago

Always in those stories
the cicadas sang

I did not know they would call me
away to their sung land
to this strange fellowship
of roads, and towns and histories

The ecstatic trees
the prostrate road

D. Dina Friedman

Bridge

My parents never crossed The Kissing Bridge.
I sat behind them in the stagnant heat.
They swerved away, sweat trickling
down their necks. I caught a flash

of lovers spread on stones, a whirl
of tongues and skin. The car approaching honked.
The sky blushed pink, then faded into dark.
We headed home. No stars, no moon.

How would they find their way
when they were done? Or would they spend the night
out in the fog? When love was false,
the bridge suspension swung,

the legend said. I didn't care.
I swore, one night I'd sneak out of my room
and curve into a body hot as stars.

Contributors

Nathaniel Blaesing is a former Louisiana Army National Guard helicopter pilot and flight instructor. He spent a year in Iraq followed closely by flying air-rescues over New Orleans following Hurricane Katrina. Now he is working to piece his life and his story together while building a nest of his own with his wife and newborn son in the tranquil city of Iowa City, Iowa.

John Blair's new poetry collection, *Playful Song Called Beautiful*, is recently published by the University of Iowa Press. He has also published five other books, including two poetry collections, *The Occasions of Paradise* (U. Tampa Press, 2012) and *The Green Girls* (Pleiades Press, 2003). He has published poems with various magazines, including *Poetry*, *The Sewanee Review*, *The Georgia Review*, and *New Letters*.

Jami Buck is an award-winning interdisciplinary artist and writer from the Mississippi Gulf Coast. Her paintings and photographs are held in private and corporate collections across the U.S. Writing has become an important tool in her exploration of the natural world and the nature of relationships. She currently lives in Mobile, Alabama.

Thomas DeConna was born in 1953 and grew up in New Jersey. After being an English teacher for thirty-nine years, he retired. He has had dozens of poems published in literary magazines. Currently, he is writing short stories and has completed a novel manuscript.

Liz Dolan's first poetry collection, *They Abide*, nominated for The McGovern Prize, Ashland University, was published by March Street. An eight-time Pushcart nominee and winner of Best of the Web, she was a finalist for Best of the Net 2014. She won The Nassau Prize for Nonfiction, 2011, and the same prize for fiction, 2015. She has received fellowships from the Delaware Division of the Arts, The Atlantic Center for the Arts and Martha's Vineyard.

Summer Edward is a writer from Trinidad. Her work has appeared or is forthcoming in *Horn Book Magazine*, *Kweli Journal*, *The Missing Slate*, *Matatu: Journal for African Culture and Society*, *Moko Magazine*, *Duende*, *The Ekphrastic Review*, *Bim: Arts for the 21st Century*, *sx salon*, *tongues of the ocean*, *The Columbia Review*, *The Caribbean Writer*, *Obsidian: Literature in the African Diaspora*, *ALTARWORK*, and others. She was thrice shortlisted for the Small Axe Literary Prize, nominated for the Pushcart Prize, and was selected for the NGC Bocas Lit Fest's New Talent Showcase, spotlighting the best emerging Caribbean writers. Her work has been anthologized in *Whaleheart:*

Journey into the Night with Maya Christina Gonzalez and 23 Courageous ArtistAuthors (Reflection Press, 2015) and *New Worlds, Old Ways: Speculative Tales from the Caribbean* (Peepal Tree Press, 2016). She is a dual citizenship holder who divides her time between Philadelphia, USA and Trinidad.

D. DINA FRIEDMAN has received two Pushcart Prize nominations and published in many journals including *Calyx, Kentucky Review, Bloodroot, Inkwell, Tsunami, The Sun, Anderbo,* and *Rhino.* Dina is also the author of two young adult novels, *Escaping Into the Night* and *Playing Dad's Song.* She has an MFA from Lesley University and teaches at the University of Massachusetts/ Amherst. http://www.ddinafriedman.com

ALICE FRIMAN's sixth full-length collection is *The View from Saturn,* LSU Press. Her previous collection is *Vinculum,* LSU, for which she won the 2012 Georgia Author of the Year Award in Poetry. She is a recipient of a Pushcart Prize, is included in *Best American Poetry,* and has just won the 2016 Paumanok Award. She's been published in *Poetry, The Georgia Review, Ploughshares, The Gettysburg Review, The Southern Review, New Letters,* etc. and in thirteen other countries. Friman lives in Milledgeville, Georgia, where was Poet-in-Residence at Georgia College. Her podcast, *Ask Alice,* can be seen on YouTube.

CAROLYN GELLAND's two collections of poems are *Dream-Shuttle* (2013) and *Four-Alarm House* (2012). Her poems, essays, and reviews have appeared in *The Notre Dame Review, Rosebud, The Anglican Theological Review, The Bitter Oleander,* and many other journals. Her marriage to the poet Kenneth Frost *(Coring the Moon: Selected Poems, 2014)* has been like living in and with a lighthouse—brilliant.

SISTER LOU ELLA HICKMAN, I.W.B.S. is a member of the Sisters of the Incarnate Word and Blessed Sacrament. She has a B.A. in elementary education and masters in theology. Sister has been a teacher of all levels including college and she has worked in two libraries. Presently she is a freelance writer as well as a certified spiritual director. Her poems and articles have been published in numerous magazines as well as a poem published in *After Shocks: Poetry of Recovery for Life-Shattering Events,* edited by Tom Lombardo, and a poem published in *Down to the Dark River* and *The Southern Quarterly,* both edited by Philp Kolin. She and Pam Edwards co-authored *Catechizing with Liturgical Symbols.* Her first book of poetry, *she: robed and wordless,* published by Press 53, was released in the fall of 2015.

RUTH KESSLER grew up in Poland and Israel. Her publications include *Fire Ashes Wings* (poems giving voice to women in myths and the arts), and some seventy poems in journals and anthologies, several of which won special distinctions. Her manuscript *The Country of Elsewheres* has been a finalist in several book contests. Her poems have been set to music and made into a limited-edition artist book. Awards include Individual NYSCA grants and Yaddo, MacDowell, VCCA, VSC, and Saltonstall fellowships. She was invited to read at the Women in Music Festival and Women and Poetry Festival, and was June's Featured Poet at Contemporary American Voices. She lives in NYC. www.RuthKessler.com

PHILIP C. KOLIN is Distinguished Professor of English (Emeritus) at the University of Southern Mississippi. He has published more than 40 books, including critical studies of Tennessee Williams, Shakespeare, Edward Albee, Adrienne Kennedy, etc. as well as eight collections of poems, the two most recent being *Emmett Till in Different States: Poems* (Third World, 2015) and *Benedict's Daughter: Poems* (Wipf and Stock, 2017). Kolin has also published a business and technical writing textbook, *Successful Writing at Work*, now in its 11th edition from Cengage Publishing.

RICHARD KOSTELANETZ's work appears in various editions of *Readers Guide to Twentieth-Century Writers*, *Merriam-Webster Encyclopedia of Literature*, *Contemporary Poets*, *Contemporary Novelists*, *Postmodern Fiction*, *Webster's Dictionary of American Writers*, *Baker's Biographical Dictionary of Musicians*, *Directory of American Scholars*, *Who's Who in America*, NNDB. com, Wikipedia, and Britannica.com, among other distinguished directories.

JENNIFER LANG's essays have appeared in *The Tishman Review*, *Pithead Chapel*, *Under the Sun*, *Ascent*, and *Hippocampus Magazine* among others. Twice nominated for a Pushcart Prize, she was a finalist in *Crab Orchard Review*'s Literary Nonfiction Contest in 2017. She holds an MFA in Writing from Vermont College of Fine Arts. She lives in Raanana, Israel with her family, but her heart and soul reside in her birthplace, the San Francisco Bay Area. Find her at http://israelwriterstudio.com and follow her on Twitter at @JenLangWrites.

PHILIP MARTIN is an award-winning short story author, having earned Second (2014) and First (2015) in the Tuscany Prize for Catholic Fiction. His other stories have been featured in *Foliate Oak*, *Eternal Remedy*, and *Remembered Arts*. He lives with his family in and writes from Daphne, AL.

WILLIAM MILLER's sixth collection of poetry, *Recovering Biker*, was published by The Edwin Mellen Press in fall 2017. His poems have appeared in *The Southern Review*, *The Penn Review*, *Shenandoah*, *West Branch*, and *Prairie Schooner*. He lives and writes in the French Quarter of New Orleans.

BENJAMIN MUELLER's poems have appeared in *Valparaiso Poetry Review*, *Two*

Hawks Quarterly, 42 Opus, Euphony, Chronogram Magazine, and *From the Finger Lakes: A Poetry Anthology.* He lives with his wife and twin toddlers in Ithaca, New York where he teaches high school English and special education.

Robbi Nester is a survivor who lives and writes in Southern California. She is the author of an ekphrastic chapbook, *Balance* (White Violet, 2012) and a collection of poems, *A Likely Story* (Moon Tide, 2014). She has also edited two anthologies, *The Liberal Media Made Me Do It!* (Nine Toes, 2014) and an e-anthology, *Over the Moon: Birds, Beasts, and Trees—celebrating the photography of Beth Moon* (accessible at http://www.poemeleon.org/over-the-moon-birds-beasts-and). Her poetry, essays, reviews, etc. have appeared in many journals and anthologies and on a number of web logs and websites.

Mary S. Palmer teaches English at Faulkner University and has published twelve books. *George Wallace: An Enigma* and the second edition of *Time Will Tell* were released in 2016 and 2017. She has won several awards for her writing and her short story, *The Concrete Block Wall,* won first place for *The Hackney Award* for 2016. She has been awarded a grant from Faulkner University to write a book entitled *New Literary Journey: Tourism Writing,* and is currently working on that project.

Lisa Rosenberg is the 2017-2018 Poet Laureate of San Mateo County, California. She holds degrees in Physics and Creative Writing, and received a Wallace Stegner Fellowship in Poetry from Stanford. She worked for many years in engineering prior to founding an independent consulting practice. Her writing appears in literary, technical, and scientific venues. Her poetry publications include *The Threepenny Review, Poetry, Witness, Southwest Review, Poetry Daily,* and *The Poetry Anthology 1912 -2002.*

Gianna Russo is the author of *Moonflower* (2011, Kitsune Books), winner of the Florida Book Award Bronze Medal and the Florida Publishers Association Silver Award. A Pushcart Prize nominee, she has had publications in literary magazines across the country and is the founding editor of the poetry chapbook publisher YellowJacket Press (www.yellowjacketpress.org). She is Instructor of English and Creative Writing at Saint Leo University.

Vivian Shipley teaches at Southern Connecticut State University where she is Distinguished Professor. *The Poet* (SLU) and *Perennial (*Negative Capability Press, Mobile, AL), nominated for the Pulitzer Prize and 2016 Paterson Poetry Prize Finalist were published in 2015. *All of Your Messages Have Been Erased, (2010, SLU)* won 2011 Paterson Award for Sustained Literary Achievement, NEPC's Sheila Motton Book Award, and CT Press Club's Prize for Best Creative Writing. Shipley won 2015's Hackney Literary Award for Poetry and has also won PSA's Lucille Medwick Prize, Robert Frost Foundation's Poetry Prize, USC's Ann Stanford Poetry Prize, Marble Faun Poetry Prize from the Faulkner Society, NEPC's Daniel Varoujan Prize and Kent State's Hart Crane Prize.

LAURENCE SNYDAL is a poet, musician and retired teacher. He has published more than a hundred poems in magazines such as *Caperock, Spillway, Columbia,* and *Steam Ticket.* His work has also appeared in many anthologies including *Visiting Frost, The Poets Grimm,* and *The Year's Best Fantasy and Horror.* Some of his poems have been performed in Baltimore and NYC. He lives in San Jose, CA, with his wife, Susan.

JANE ST. CLAIR has published short fiction for adults in literary magazines such as *Brain.Child, Rosebud, J Journal, Thema, 34th Parallel, descant, Clockwatch Review, QWF, Clare, Thematic Magazine,* and *Red Rock Review.* Her fiction appears in several literary anthologies, including *Times of Grace, Times of Sorrow,* published by the University of Nebraska; *Mourning Sickness* from Omni Press; a collection of the best sports fiction from Main Street Rag Bookstore and a 2014 collection from Fiction Attic. She is the 2007 winner of the True Life Story contest, the 2006 first place winner of The Writers Network contest, American Accolades (first place), Hollywood's Next Success, the fourth place winner of the 2015 Tom Howard/John Reid Essay Contest, and the 2005 winner in television writing for Scriptapalooza. *Walk Me to Midnight,* her first novel, was published in 2008 by Oak Tara Press, a small POD start-up house. She is also the author of twenty-one children's books and over fifty children's short stories published through the University of Arkansas.

KEVIN STEIN has published eleven books of poetry. His books include the collections *Wrestling Li Po for the Remote* (Fifth Star Press), *Sufficiency of the Actual* (University of Illinois Press), *American Ghost Roses* (winner of the Society of Midland Authors Poetry Prize), and the essays *Poetry's Afterlife: Verse in the Digital Age* (University of Michigan Press). Recipient of grants from the NEA and the NEH, he teaches at Bradley University.

WALLY SWIST's books include *Huang Po and the Dimensions of Love* (Southern Illinois University Press, 2012); *The Daodejing: A New Interpretation,* with David Breeden and Steven Schroeder (Lamar University Press, 2015); *Invocation* (Lamar University Press, 2015), and *The Windbreak Pine* (Snapshot Press, 2016). Forthcoming books include: *The View of the River* (Kelsay Books, 2017), *Candling the Eggs* (Shanti Arts, LLC, 2017), and *Singing for Nothing from Street to Street: Selected Nonfiction as Literary Memoir* (The Operating System, 2018).

MARIA TERRONE is the author of the poetry collections *Eye to Eye* (Bordighera Press); *A Secret Room in Fall* (McGovern Prize, Ashland Poetry Press); *The Bodies We Were Loaned* (The Word Works); and a chapbook, *American Gothic, Take 2*. Her work, which has been published in French and Farsi and nominated four times for a Pushcart Prize, has appeared in magazines including *Poetry, Ploughshares* and *The Hudson Review* and in more than twenty-five anthologies. In 2016 she became poetry editor of the journal *Italian Americana*.

T.K. THORNE retired as a captain of the Birmingham Police Department and, in a second career, as executive director of a downtown business improvement district. Both experiences and a Masters in Social Work feed her fiction, poetry, and non-fiction, all of which have garnered awards. Her novels—*Noah's Wife* and *Angels At The Gate*—won national historical fiction awards, including ForeWord Review's "Book of the Year," IBPA's Benjamin Franklin, and an IPPY award. Her debut nonfiction, *Last Chance for Justice: How Relentless Investigators Uncovered New Evidence Convicting the Birmingham Church Bombers*, made the *New York Post's* list of "Books You Should Be Reading." A short film from her screenplay, "Six Blocks Wide," was a finalist in a film festival in Italy and has shown at other juried festivals in the U.S. and Europe. Most recently, she is working on a second civil rights history and delving into the world of paranormal thriller. She writes on an Alabama mountain with two dogs and a cat vying for her lap. Learn more about her at TK@tkthorne.com.

RODNEY TORRESON, Poet Laureate of Grand Rapids, Michigan from 2007-2010, is the author of two full-length books of poetry and two chapbooks. His most recent, a chapbook titled *The Secrets of Fieldwork*, was published by Finishing Line Press, in 2010. His work has appeared in such places as the *Beloit Poetry Journal, Margie, Poetry Lore*, and *Spillway*. In addition, he has new poems forthcoming in *Great Lakes Review, Naugatuck River Review*, and *Third Coast*.

SARAH BROWN WEITZMAN has had work in hundreds of journals and anthologies including *Miramar, The New Ohio Review, Poet & Critic, The North American Review, Rattle, Mid-American Review, Ekphrasis, Poet Lore, Spillway*, etc. Sarah received a Fellowship from the National Endowment for the Arts. A departure from poetry, her fourth book, *Herman and the Ice Witch*, is a children's novel published by Main Street Rag. Her latest chapbook, *Looking Back*, is forthcoming from Finishing Line Press.

ROY WHITE is a blind person who lives in Saint Paul, Minnesota with a lovely woman and a handsome dog. His poems and essays have appeared in *BOAAT Journal, Tinderbox, Lascaux Review*, and elsewhere, and he blogs at lippenheimer. wordpress.com.

www.ingramcontent.com/pod-product-compliance
Lightning Source LLC
Chambersburg PA
CBHW050351030726
47503CB00008B/2728